Gordon Ramsay's
Great Escape

Food Mark Sargeant Text Emily Quah Photographer Emma Lee
Reportage Photography Jonathan Gregson Art Director Patrick Budge
Props Stylist Emma Thomas

HarperCollins*Publishers*

Cook's notes

Spoon measures are level, unless otherwise specified:
1 tsp is equivalent to 5ml; 1 tbsp is equivalent to 15ml.

Use good-quality sea salt, freshly ground pepper and fresh herbs for the best flavour.

Use large eggs unless otherwise suggested, ideally organic or free-range. If you are pregnant or in a vulnerable health group, avoid dishes using raw egg whites or lightly cooked eggs.

Individual ovens may vary in actual temperature by 10° from the setting, so it is important to know your oven. Use an oven thermometer to check its accuracy.

Timings are provided as guidelines, with a description of colour or texture where appropriate, but readers should rely on their own judgement as to when a dish is properly cooked.

10 9 8 7 6 5 4 3 2 1

HarperCollins*Publishers*
77–85 Fulham Palace Road,
Hammersmith, London W6 8JB
www.harpercollins.co.uk

First published by HarperCollins*Publishers* 2010

Text © 2010 Gordon Ramsay
Food Photography © 2010 Emma Lee
Reportage Photography © 2010 Jonathan Gregson

Gordon Ramsay asserts the moral right to be identified as the author of this work

A CIP catalogue record of this book is available from the British Library

ISBN 978-0-00-787663-1

Printed and bound in China by
South China Printing Company Ltd

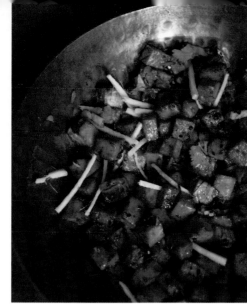

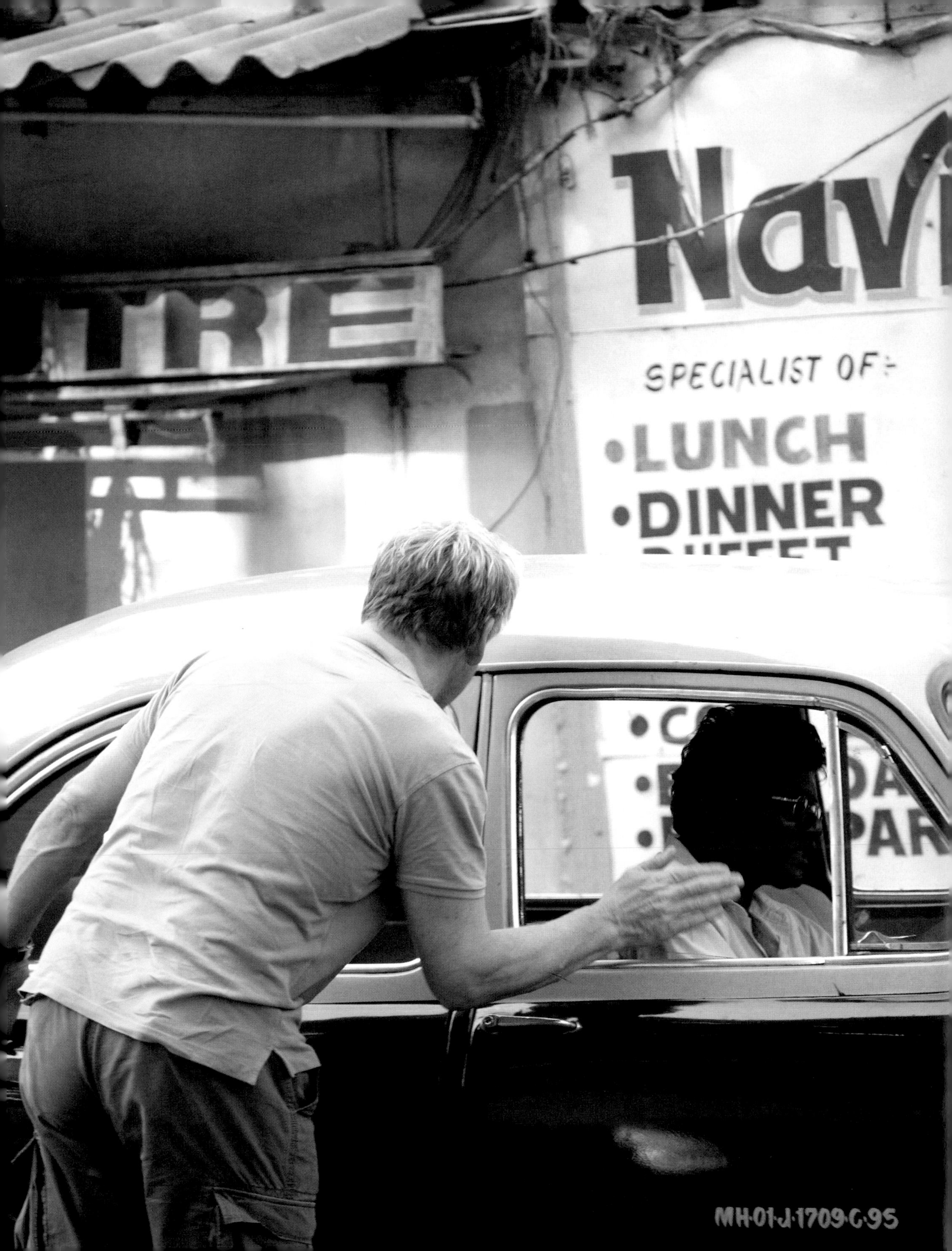
TRE
SPECIALIST OF:-
•LUNCH
•DINNER
MH-01-J-1709-C-95

Contents

Introduction

Over 3.5 million curries are eaten in the UK each year, which shows how much Indian cuisine is now part and parcel of the British diet. My own love affair with Indian food started when my mother made me my first curry as a child. Granted, mum's inauthentic curries were nothing like what we're used to today – hers were mostly flavoured with curry powder with the occasional handful of sultanas thrown in – but to us the flavours seemed exotic and mesmerising and I was hooked.

Since I left home and started working, Friday-night curries have become a ritual. Like most people, I have had favourite dishes, which I would order time and again, but overall I felt pretty comfortable with the food and thought that I knew quite a bit about Indian cuisine. How wrong I was! I had never been to India before this trip, and what little I knew about the country and its food was based on general stereotypes and preconceptions. I now realise that it is impossible to summarise the food of a vast subcontinent where differing cultures, religion, topography, climate and history all influence what food is eaten and how it is cooked.

When the opportunity came for a culinary adventure in India, the choice was simple. This was the chance of a lifetime to escape from the grind of daily life and discover the truth about Indian cuisine. I knew that real Indian food was not to be found in fancy restaurants and hotel eateries; instead I had to travel the country and eat as ordinary Indians do, regardless of caste, class or religious differences.

My journey started in the north, in the capital of New Delhi, home to 17 million residents. As I entered the city the first thing that struck me was the sheer contrast of wealth and severe poverty that was apparent everywhere, but I soon noticed that no matter what the individual situation was, almost everyone had a beaming smile. The Delhi residents also seemed to be working constantly, day and night; however, amid the hustle and bustle, I got a real sense of organised chaos that I had never experienced anywhere else before. In fact, this was the feeling I got in almost every Indian city to which I travelled, but Old Delhi was certainly a culture shock. The sights at the Red Fort were wonderful, and there were beautiful temples everywhere you looked, but, in the middle of it all, I was amazed to see rows of fragile-looking shacks that sold everything from mobile phones and shoes to food and Honda motorbikes!

Navigating and crossing the streets of Delhi proved to be a big challenge. The roads were filled with maniacs who drove wherever they chose with utter disregard for any street signs, regulations or pedestrians! There was a constant echo of horns beeping the whole time as every driver felt that he had the right of way. For me, the most amusing sight had to be the occasional herd of cows meandering along the streets, oblivious to oncoming traffic, while taxis, cars, motorbikes and tuk tuks did their best to avoid hitting the sacred animals.

Where food was concerned, my most memorable meal in Delhi was at the legendary Moti Mahal restaurant in Daryaganj, where classics such as tandoori chicken and butter chicken (one of my all-time favourites) were invented over 60 years ago. It was here that I met Seema Chandra, a renowned food writer and critic, who explained to me that the food in India is truly different from the Indian food that you get in Britain. This was clearly evident in the dishes at Moti Mahal: the delicious butter chicken was very moist, tender and flavoursome – unlike anything I've ever tasted. According to Seema, real Indian food is found on the streets and in family homes. Indians have not historically had a big restaurant culture, although this has now changed, and (for those who can afford it) eating out has become a popular pastime. Many homes have servants or mothers and grandmothers who prepare fresh, delicious meals for the entire family three times a day. Workers who do not have time to go home for lunch pick up cheap, delicious street food to sustain them until they can get home for dinner; children bring their lunches to school carefully packed in multi-tiered tiffin carriers, and shoppers indulge in street snacks before going home for their main meals. This emphasis on traditional home cooking means that recipes have been passed down from generation to generation and have seldom been well recorded, so if I wanted to get a true flavour of Indian cookery, I needed to roll up my sleeves and get my hands dirty.

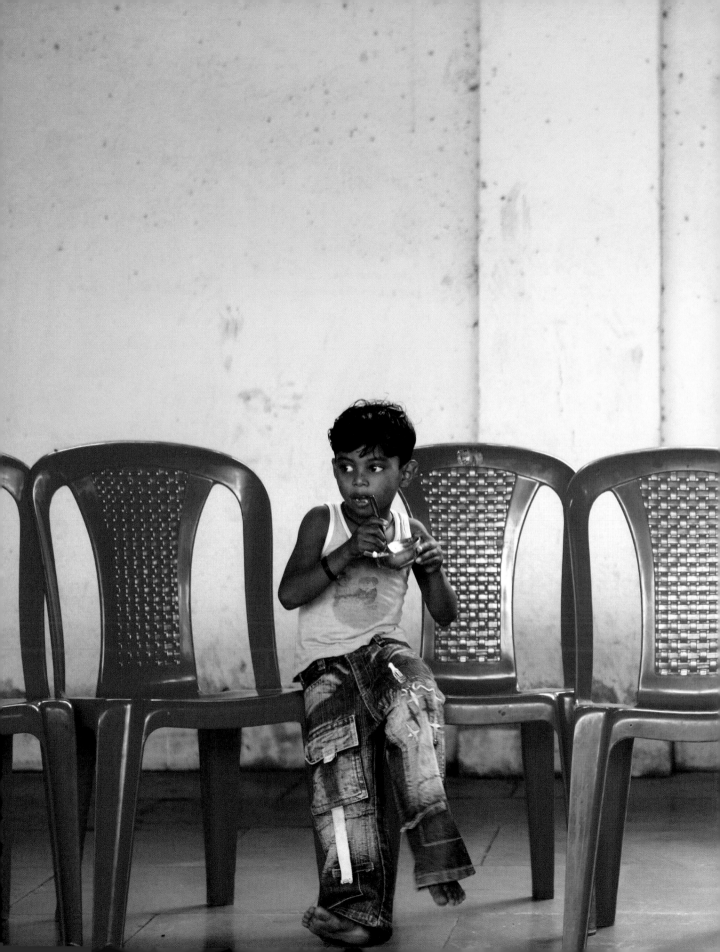

One of the first things I learnt was that food is very important in India. Even the very poor will find a way to eat well with cheap but delicious meals. I understood this on board the Mangalore Express, on my way to Lucknow, the foremost city of food and culture. To earn my fare I was given an apron and immediately set on the task of prepping vegetables in the train cafeteria. There, a team of five chefs and 20 waiters make and serve fresh meals to over 400 passengers each day. For an equivalent of £110 a month, the chefs work 10 hours a day, 6 days a week in the most challenging of work environments. Pots constantly rattled and the portable stove shifted with the movements of the train. Nonetheless, they took great care to produce

This simple and honest approach to food was echoed in Nagaland and Assam, two of the Seven Sister States I visited in the remote northeastern corner of India. Dried spices, so ubiquitous in mainstream Indian cooking, are virtually absent from recipes there; instead, fresh chillies, ginger and garlic are the predominant flavourings. Meat and fish are hunted and cooked on the bone, resulting in very little wastage, and every part of an animal is eaten. I was also intrigued by the prevalent use of bamboo shoots in Nagaland, both in the fresh, smoked and dried forms, which link the cuisine to those of neighbouring China and Myanmar. Naturally, rice is the staple food of the region, and it comes in various forms. A local favourite is glutinous rice roasted in segments of fresh bamboo over an open fire. Talk about low-impact eco-cooking!

Next, my travels took me to the coastal areas of Kerala. With its beautiful and lush waterways, it is a much calmer and more relaxed part of India – exactly what I needed after an exhausting couple of weeks criss-crossing the country. Naturally, rice and fish are their staples, but as there is a sizeable Syrian Christian population in the area, pork and beef were also back on the menu. The food is lighter, as coconut milk is used in place of butter and cream, and more fragrant with the liberal use of spices and fresh curry leaves. One of the tastiest dishes I tried was *karimeen pollichathu* (see page 70). Karimeen is a much loved local freshwater fish, dubbed the 'Fish of Kerala', and in this dish it is smothered with a spice paste and roasted in banana leaves. The fish had a sublime flavour that reminded me of a sweet Dover sole; it is a real shame we can't get it in England.

No trip to Kerala is complete without a visit to a spice market, and I was extremely impressed with the multi-coloured markets of Cochin. The image of giant piles of ginger, turmeric, cinnamon, cardamom and saffron (as well as the intoxicating fragrance) will always be embedded

Glossary

Ajwain – Also known as carom seeds, ajwain resemble small cumin seeds but they have a strong fragrance of thyme and a slightly bitter and pungent flavour. They are always roasted in the oven or fried in oil or butter in Indian cooking.

Amchur/Amchoor – Green mango powder made by grinding pitted unripe mangoes that have been left to dry out in the sun. It has a greyish colour and a distinctive tart flavour, hence its use as a souring agent for food. It does not require cooking but may be added to dishes or sprinkled over snacks in place of lemon juice or vinegar.

Asafoetida (*Hing/Heeng* in Hindi) – A spice made from the resinous gum of the *Ferula assafoetida* plant. Mostly sold in powdered form, asafoetida is used in tiny quantities as a digestive aid to fight off indigestion and flatulence. It is often added to dishes at the beginning of the cooking process to be cooked out with other spices. Raw asafoetida has a very pungent, rather disagreeable odour that seems to disappear once cooked to leave a mellow, slightly sweet tang that is similar to that of roasted onions and garlic. Because it is not widely sold in super-markets and you would only use a pinch in any dish, I have made it optional in the recipes here.

Atta/Chapatti flour – A wholewheat flour rich in fibre and protein that is used to make many classic unleavened Indian breads, such as chapatti and paratha. It can be bought from specialist Indian shops and some major supermarkets. If you can't find it, use equal quantities of wholemeal and plain flours.

Chaat masala – A dry spice blend with a distinctive sour flavour that is mostly used as a condiment. It is often sprinkled over Indian snacks, raw fruit salads and tandoori dishes, and it can also be used to 'liven' up fruit juices. The specific blend of spices may vary according to the brand (or individual tastes) but chaat masala usually consists of dried mango powder, dried ginger, black salt, ground dried mint and asafoetida. Ready-made packets are widely available at Asian grocers.

Chai – A generic Hindi word for tea, but outside of India chai is commonly used to imply masala chai, a popular Indian-spiced milk tea.

Channa dal – Also known as *cholar dal* in Bengali, these are skinned and split black gram – they look and taste similar to yellow split peas, but the grains are marginally smaller. They have an earthy and nutty flavour. If you can't get hold of them, use yellow split peas instead.

Coconut oil – An oil used commonly in southern Indian cooking that has been extracted from coconuts by a process of distillation. It is white in colour when solid but becomes transparent when heated. It has a high burning point, which makes it suitable for frying foods. It is high in saturated fats, and so for health reasons some people prefer to substitute it with other vegetable oils.

Garam masala – An aromatic spice blend that is used both during the cooking process, for a subtle fragrance, and as a garnish, where it is lightly sprinkled over a finished dish to give an added burst of aroma and flavour. *Garam* means 'warming' or 'hot' and the blend commonly includes cardamom seeds, cumin or black cumin seeds, nutmeg, black peppercorns, cloves and cinnamon, coriander and fennel seeds, although recipes vary significantly from region to region. Ready-made garam masala is easily found in supermarkets and Asian shops, but some brands tend to bulk up the ingredients with cheaper spices such as ground cumin and coriander.

Ghee – This is essentially clarified butter, which features heavily in northern Indian cooking. You can buy it ready-made in tins at Asian grocers, but I find these have a strong, overpowering aroma. To clarify butter, melt it gently, then pour off the oil through a muslin-lined sieve and discard the milky solids. For health reasons, many Indians now mainly cook with vegetable oil, but they will add a little unsalted butter or ghee to flavour and enrich a dish.

Gram flour – Also known as *besan*, this is made from finely ground chickpeas or channa dal. It is used in Indian cooking for a variety of purposes, such as soups and curries, and it is an integral part of the batter for bhajis and pakoras.

Grated coconut – Freshly grated coconut is often called for in Indian cooking. To extract the flesh from a coconut, crack it with the back of a strong cleaver or using a hammer. Drain off the coconut water (or save to drink later). You should have two halves of the coconut. Prise out the white flesh with a strong spoon then finely shred or grate using a food processor. Grated coconut can be frozen successfully for at least a month.

Jaggery – An unrefined natural sugar made from the concentrated sap of the date palm. It lends a distinctive sweet taste to both sweet and savoury dishes. Usually sold in solid blocks, jaggery is often grated before it is incorporated into dishes. The darker the colour of the jaggery, the stronger the flavour. You can substitute it with palm sugar or light brown soft sugar.

Kalonji – Also known as nigella seeds, these are black onion seeds with a tear-drop shape. Kalonji is frequently used in pickles, chutneys and fish dishes as well as sprinkled on to Indian flat breads.

Karahi – A large, all-purpose rounded pan that is an essential piece of equipment in an Indian kitchen. It is particularly useful for deep-frying as it allows you to use less oil than you would when using a regular saucepan. If you do not already own a karahi, a wok makes a very good substitute.

Mustard oil – The oil extracted from mustard seeds, this has a pungent and slightly bitter taste when raw. Once heated, it develops a distinctive sweet flavour. An acquired taste, it is most commonly used in Bengali cooking for pickling and cooking fish and vegetables. If you can't find it, substitute it with vegetable or groundnut oil.

Panch phoran – A Bengali spice blend made up of equal quantities of whole fennel seeds, fenugreek seeds, black mustard seeds, cumin seeds and nigella or black onion seeds.

Paneer – This fresh, unsalted curd cheese is widely used in both sweet and savoury Indian dishes. Paneer is very easy to make, requiring only whole milk and either lemon juice or vinegar. The milk is heated almost to boiling point, then removed from the heat and a little lemon juice or vinegar is stirred in. The milk will curdle or separate, and at this point the liquid is strained and hung for a few hours to remove the watery whey, leaving behind the fresh curd. Paneer is best made on the day it is to be eaten.

Rosewater – Made from distilled rose petals, rosewater is produced as a by-product of the process used to make rose oil. The widespread use of rosewater in Indian cooking comes from Persian influence; it is commonly sprinkled over biryani or pilau rice to lend a perfumed aroma to the dish.

Tamarind – Used as a souring agent in Indian cooking, particularly in the south, tamarind pulp is usually sold in blocks. To get tamarind purée, soak the tamarind pulp in water (roughly double the volume of water to weight of pulp) for at least 30 minutes. You should break the tamarind block up with your hands to achieve maximum flavour before straining the purée through a sieve and discarding the husks. More convenient but less flavour-some ready-made tamarind paste is now widely sold in jars in major supermarkets.

Tuvar dal – Dark ochre-coloured split and skinned pigeon pea lentils with a mild nutty and earthy flavour. These versatile lentils are very popular in Indian cooking and are a good source of protein and fibre.

Urad dal – Black gram usually sold split and skinned to reveal the yellow lentils inside. Urad dal is ground with rice to make the classic southern Indian dosa. It is also often fried in small quantities to give a nutty crunch to vegetable or rice dishes.

Starters & snacks

Malai chicken kebabs

These Punjabi chicken kebabs come from the north-west of India and are traditionally cooked in a hot tandoor. The kebabs are fairly mild, which makes them suitable for serving to a young family. To turn them into a main meal, serve with fluffy basmati rice or soft flat breads such as *puri* or *naan*, a sweet and sour chutney and some side vegetable dishes.

Cut the chicken into 2.5–3cm cubes. In a large bowl, mix together all the ingredients for the marinade and season well with salt and pepper. Add the chicken pieces to the marinade and mix well to ensure that every piece is well coated. Cover the bowl with cling film and chill for a few hours, preferably overnight.

Soak 6–8 bamboo skewers in cold water for at least 20 minutes. When ready to cook, heat the grill to the highest setting. Halve the peppers and remove and discard the seeds. Cut the peppers into small cubes the same size as the chicken pieces. Thread the chicken pieces and peppers alternately on to the soaked bamboo skewers and place on a lightly oiled baking tray. Grill for about 8–10 minutes, basting, turning and basting again with the ghee or butter a couple of times during cooking. The chicken should be just firm when lightly pressed.

Serve the chicken kebabs on shredded lettuce leaves with a few lemon wedges and a raita on the side.

SERVES 4–6
500g boneless and skinless chicken breasts
sea salt and freshly ground black pepper
6–8 bamboo skewers
1 red pepper
1 yellow or orange pepper
2 tbsp ghee or melted unsalted butter

MARINADE
150ml double cream or soured cream
2 cardamom pods, split and seeds finely crushed
3cm ginger, peeled and finely grated
3 large garlic cloves, peeled and finely crushed
2 tbsp gram flour
1 tsp garam masala
1 tsp dried mango powder
1 tsp ground cumin
½ tsp ground turmeric
2 mild green chillies, deseeded and finely chopped

SERVES 4

500g tomatoes

2 tbsp vegetable oil

1 large onion, peeled and chopped

2.5cm ginger, peeled and chopped

2 large garlic cloves, peeled and chopped

sea salt and freshly ground black pepper

2 red chillies, deseeded and finely chopped

½ tsp dried fenugreek, crushed with a pinch of salt

1 bay leaf

1 tsp ground turmeric

1 tsp ground cumin

100g tomato purée

400ml tin coconut milk

pinch of sugar (optional)

1 tbsp coconut or vegetable oil

1 tsp cumin seeds

pinch of asafoetida (optional)

handful of coriander leaves and 2 tbsp toasted flaked coconut, to garnish (optional)

Spiced tomato and coconut soup

This is my take on *rasam*, a spicy South Indian tomato soup, which is generally served with rice as a second course, following an appetising dish of *sambar* (see page 213). It is thought that our much loved mulligatawny soup is a derivative of rasam, although we have, through the years, toned down the heat level to suit tamer British palates. For this soup, it is better to use cheap cooking tomatoes that are flavourful but slightly sour, as this provides an astringency to balance the slightly sweet and creamy coconut milk.

Bring a pan of water to the boil. Lightly score a cross at the top and base of each tomato then lower them into the boiling water for 15–20 seconds. Remove with a slotted spoon and refresh in a bowl of iced water. Once cooled, peel off the skins of the tomato and roughly chop the flesh. Set aside.

Heat the oil in a medium saucepan and add the onion, ginger and garlic. Add a pinch of salt and some pepper and sweat for 4–5 minutes until the onion begins to soften. Add the chillies, fenugreek, bay leaf, turmeric and cumin and cook for another 3–4 minutes. Tip in the chopped tomatoes and tomato purée and stir well.

Pour in the coconut milk and use the tin to measure out an equal amount of water. Add this to the pan and bring to a simmer. Cook gently for about 15–20 minutes until the tomatoes are very soft and have broken down.

Purée the soup using a stick blender (or an ordinary one) and if you want a really smooth result, push the purée through a fine sieve into a clean pan. Season well to taste with salt and black pepper, adding a pinch of sugar if it tastes too acidic from the tomatoes. If you prefer a thinner soup, dilute it with some boiling water and adjust the seasoning.

When you are ready to serve, reheat the soup. In a small saucepan, heat the coconut or vegetable oil and add the cumin seeds and asafoetida, if using. As they begin to pop, take the pan off the heat and pour the spiced oil into the tomato soup. Stir well.

Ladle into warm bowls and garnish with coriander leaves and toasted flaked coconut, if you wish. Serve immediately.

Spicy prawn pakoras

I like to think of pakoras as the Indian equivalent of the Japanese tempura. They typically consist of fish, meat or vegetables that are coated in a batter made from spiced gram (chickpea) flour and then deep-fried until golden brown. These prawn pakoras are especially delicious with a Spicy green or Tomato and cucumber chutney (see pages 215 and 224).

Shell and devein the prawns, leaving the tails intact. Place them in a bowl and toss with the chopped chillies and garlic.

Next, make the batter by mixing the flour, salt and spices together in a large bowl. Make a well in the centre and add just enough of the warm water to form a thick, smooth paste with a slow-dropping consistency. Leave to stand for a few minutes.

Preheat the oven to the lowest setting and heat 6cm of oil in a karahi or deep saucepan to 170–180°C. One at a time, hold the prawns by their tails, dip them in the spicy batter mix to coat, then drop them into the hot oil. Fry for 3–4 minutes, turning once, until crisp and golden brown all over. Drain on a baking tray lined with kitchen paper and keep warm in the oven while you cook the rest. Serve immediately while they are still hot.

SERVES 4

350g raw prawns, shell on
2 green chillies, deseeded and very finely chopped
3 garlic cloves, peeled and finely crushed
vegetable oil, for deep-frying

BATTER

150g gram (or plain) flour
½ tsp sea salt
½ tsp ground turmeric
½ tsp cumin seeds
½ tsp ground coriander
½ tsp garam masala
100–125ml warm water

SERVES 4

450g prawns, peeled
  and deveined
sea salt and freshly
  ground black pepper
handful of coriander
  leaves and stalks
2 medium onions,
  peeled and very finely
  chopped
2 green chillies,
  deseeded and finely
  chopped
75g dried breadcrumbs
vegetable oil, for
  shallow-frying

SAUCE

1 tbsp vegetable oil
20g unsalted butter
1 large onion, peeled
  and finely chopped
3cm ginger, peeled and
  finely grated
2 tsp garam masala
1 heaped tsp ground
  turmeric
400ml tin coconut milk
150ml water

Prawn koftas

These delectable prawn koftas are served with a lightly spiced sauce, which is delicious soaked up with warm flat breads. They can be eaten as a side dish, but I like them as a substantial snack.

Put the prawns in a food processor along with a pinch each of salt and pepper. Finely chop the coriander stalks, saving the leaves to garnish the dish. Add the chopped stems to the food processor along with a third of the onions. Pulse the ingredients for a few seconds until the prawns are finely chopped but not puréed.

Transfer to a bowl and stir in the remaining onions and chopped chillies. Fry a small ball of the mixture and taste to check the seasoning. Using wet hands, roll the mixture into walnut-sized balls and coat them in the breadcrumbs.

Heat 4cm of oil in a wide pan until hot. In batches, fry the prawn koftas until golden brown all over, turning once halfway. Lift them out with a slotted spoon and drain on a plate lined with kitchen paper.

To make the sauce, heat the vegetable oil and butter in a saucepan. Add the onion, ginger and a pinch of salt and sauté for 3–4 minutes. Add the garam masala and turmeric and stir frequently for another 3–4 minutes to cook out the rawness of the spice. Pour in the coconut milk and water and bring to a simmer. Cook until the sauce has reduced by a third and thickened.

Add the prawn koftas to the pan and gently stir once to coat them in the sauce. Simmer for a few minutes until they are heated through. Transfer to a warm bowl and serve garnished with coriander leaves.

Maharashtrian white bean patties

These little bean cakes, called *pavta* patties, are generally made with dried lima beans in India, but as these are hard to find here, use any other white bean. To save time, you can use tinned beans, but they are no match for the flavour and texture of dried ones.

Drain the beans and place in a saucepan with 1 litre of water. Bring to the boil and skim off the surface froth. Reduce the heat and simmer for 1–1½ hours until the beans are soft but not mushy. Drain well, reserving a little cooking water, and tip into a food processor. Blend to a fine purée, adding a little reserved water as necessary. Set aside.

Heat half the oil in a pan and add the mustard seeds. When they begin to pop, add the onion and seasoning. Sweat over a medium heat, stirring occasionally, for 4–6 minutes until the onion is soft. Add the turmeric, garam masala, cayenne pepper or chilli powder, ground coriander and asafoetida, if using. Fry for a few minutes until the spices are fragrant. Add the remaining oil and the potato and stir. Add a splash of water and cover the pan. Steam for 8–10 minutes over a low-to-medium heat, stirring once or twice, until the potatoes are soft. Tip in the puréed beans and chopped coriander. Lightly mash together using a potato masher. Taste and adjust the seasoning. If the mixture is too wet, add a little flour to get a fairly stiff dough. Leave to cool.

Shape the mixture into small fishcake-like patties and dust with a little flour. Heat a thin layer of oil in a wide frying pan until hot. In batches, fry the patties for 4–5 minutes until golden brown all over. Drain on kitchen paper and serve warm with a sweet-and-sour chutney.

MAKES 8–10

150g dried white beans (such as haricot or butter beans), soaked in water overnight
4 tbsp vegetable oil, plus extra for frying
1 tsp black mustard seeds
1 small onion, peeled and finely chopped
sea salt and freshly ground black pepper
1 tsp ground turmeric
½ tsp garam masala
½ tsp cayenne pepper (or chilli powder), to taste
1 tsp ground coriander
pinch of asafoetida (optional)
1 large potato, about 300g, peeled and diced
handful of coriander leaves, chopped
1–2 tbsp plain flour, plus extra to dust

MAKES 12–14

1 tsp fine sea salt

1 tsp ground turmeric

1 tsp cayenne pepper

¼ tsp freshly ground
black pepper

1 medium aubergine,
about 350g, cut in half
lengthways then into
1cm cubes

1 tbsp vegetable oil,
plus extra for
deep-frying

1 medium onion, peeled
and finely chopped

BATTER

150g gram (or plain)
flour

½ tsp fine sea salt

1 tsp ground turmeric

1 tsp toasted cumin
seeds

75–100ml warm water

Aubergine bhajis

We are most familiar with onion bhajis here in the UK, and these aubergine fritters are a delicious alternative. The word *bhajia*, literally meaning 'fried', has been anglicised to the *bhaji* or *bhajee* that we recognise today. The fritters are made with a batter very similar to that used to make pakoras, but here it does not coat the main ingredient, instead the vegetable is finely chopped and mixed through the batter. You can try making the fritters with other vegetables such as courgettes, cauliflower or even okra.

First, make the batter by combining the flour, salt, turmeric and cumin seeds in a large bowl. Gradually stir in enough water to get a thick batter with a slow-dropping consistency. Leave to stand for a few minutes while you prepare the vegetables.

In a small bowl, combine the salt, turmeric, cayenne and black pepper. Sprinkle this over the aubergine and toss to coat. Heat a tablespoon of oil in a large pan and sauté the onion with a pinch of seasoning for 6–8 minutes until golden brown. Add the aubergine and cook for 3–4 minutes or until it has softened. Remove the pan from the heat and cool slightly.

Tip the aubergine and onion mixture into the batter and mix well. Preheat the oven to the lowest setting and heat 6cm of oil in a deep saucepan (or deep-fryer) to 180°C. Gently drop spoonfuls of the bhaji mixture into the hot oil and fry in batches for 4–6 minutes until evenly golden brown and crisp. Drain on a baking tray lined with kitchen paper and keep warm while you fry the rest. Serve hot and crisp with Sweet tamarind and Spicy green chutneys (see pages 217 and 215).

Spicy vegetable and paneer wraps

SERVES 4

200g spinach leaves
2–3 tbsp vegetable oil
3cm ginger, peeled and
    finely grated
3 garlic cloves, peeled
    and finely chopped
1 green chilli, deseeded
    and finely chopped
1 small red onion,
    peeled and sliced
1 red pepper, cut into
    thin strips
2 carrots, peeled and
    cut into thin strips
1 tsp sea salt
1 tsp garam masala
1 tsp hot chilli powder
½ tsp ground cumin
225g block of paneer,
    cut into thin strips
2 tbsp chopped
    coriander
juice of ½ lemon
4 chapattis (see page
    183) or flour tortillas
Coriander and chilli
    raita (see page 202)

Vegetable wraps are typical street foods in India, particularly in busy cities like Calcutta where the notion of grabbing a cheap, nutritious, convenient snack is always appealing. If you prefer a non-vegetarian version or a more substantial filling, add cooked mince or spicy chicken pieces. This would also make a lovely lunch with a fresh and zingy salad.

Bring a pan of salted water to the boil. Add the spinach and blanch for 30 seconds to 1 minute until wilted. Drain well and set aside.

Heat the oil in a large frying pan over a medium heat. Add the ginger, garlic, chilli and onion and cook for 2–3 minutes, stirring frequently. Add the red pepper and carrots and stir well. After a few minutes, add the salt, garam masala, chilli powder and cumin. Continue to fry until the vegetables have slightly softened yet still retain some bite. Lastly, stir through the strips of paneer, chopped coriander and lemon juice and cook for a few minutes. Remove the pan from the hob.

Warm the chapattis in a wide, dry frying pan to soften them a little. (This makes them easier to wrap with.) Spread a tablespoon of Coriander and chilli raita on each warmed chapatti and cover with a layer of blanched spinach. Spoon the vegetable and paneer filling on top and roll up the chapatti to enclose the filling, as you would a parcel.

Wrap each spicy vegetable wrap in baking parchment and foil (or old newspaper) and serve warm. If you find the wraps have gone cold, warm them through in a hot oven for a few minutes before serving.

Aloo dahi puri

These little crispy filled puris are what I consider to be the ultimate *chaat* – a Hindi word that describes the various savoury delicacies that tempt passers-by to the roadside food carts found in every Indian city. You will need to make a trip to your nearest Indian grocer to secure a box of ready-made mini *pani puri* shells and a bag of *sev mamra* (crispy snacks consisting of a mixture of puffed rice, fried yellow gram noodles and spiced peanuts). Thereafter, it will only take minutes to assemble these delicious bite-sized treats.

First, prepare the potato filling. Peel and cut the potato into large chunks then boil in a pan of salted water for 10–15 minutes until tender. Drain well, then chop the potato into a small dice. Place in a bowl and mix with the chilli powder, cumin, garam masala, dried mango powder, onion, yoghurt and seasoning to taste.

When you are about ready to eat, carefully break the top of each puri to make a small hole that is big enough to add the potato filling through. (The puris are very delicate so you do need to be gentle with them.) Fill each puri with some potato mixture and a drizzle each of yoghurt and tamarind chutney. Garnish with the chopped coriander and sev mamra or sev. Serve immediately.

SERVES 4

12 ready-made pani puri shells (also known as *golgappa*)

150ml natural yoghurt

6–8 tbsp Sweet tamarind chutney (see page 217)

handful of coriander, leaves chopped, and handful of *sev mamra* (or plain sev), to garnish

POTATO FILLING

1 large waxy potato, about 250–300g

½ tsp red chilli powder

¼ tsp ground cumin

¼ tsp garam masala

½ tsp dried mango powder

1 small onion, peeled and finely diced

200ml natural yoghurt, mixed with 2–3 tbsp water

fine sea salt and freshly ground black pepper

Fish

Bengali prawn curry

Hyderabadi squid tamatar

Spiced fish wrapped in banana leaves

Fish tenga

Baked whole sea bass with green masala paste

Majuli fishcakes with tomato relish

Monkfish moilee

Tuna vattichathu

Goan fish ambotik

Dry crab curry

Grilled snapper with dry spices

Crispy battered fish with spiced okra and aubergine

Mackerel masala

Pan-fried John Dory with hot-spiced red curry sauce

Bengali prawn curry

SERVES 4

400g large raw prawns, shell on
½ tsp ground turmeric
sea salt
2 onions, peeled and roughly chopped
2cm ginger, peeled and roughly chopped
3 garlic cloves, peeled and roughly chopped
2 green chillies, deseeded and chopped
2 tbsp vegetable oil
2 tsp mustard seeds
½ tsp hot chilli powder
2 whole cloves
4 green cardamom pods
1 cinnamon stick
2 bay leaves
1 whole dried chilli
400ml tin coconut milk

This prawn curry is considered a classic dish, and marinating seafood or meat with a combination of salt and turmeric is characteristic of Bengali cooking. I love how the complementary sweetness of the prawns and coconut is contrasted with the heat and pungency of the chillies and mustard seeds. Needless to say, very fresh prawns are essential for this recipe.

Shell and devein the prawns, leaving the tails on, if you wish. Place them in a bowl with the turmeric and a pinch of salt. Mix well, then leave to marinate for 5–10 minutes. Meanwhile, put the onions, ginger, garlic and chillies into a food processor with 2 tablespoons of water. Blend to a fine wet paste.

Heat the oil in a large pan. Add the mustard seeds, chilli powder, cloves, cardamom, cinnamon, bay leaves and whole chilli. Fry for 1–2 minutes until the spices become fragrant and the mustard seeds begin to sputter. Add the wet paste to the pan and fry over a low heat for 12–15 minutes, stirring frequently.

Add the coconut milk to the pan and bring to a simmer over a low heat. Add the prawns and simmer for 2–3 minutes, until they are opaque and just cooked through. Transfer to a warm bowl and serve immediately with warm Indian breads or rice.

Hyderabadi squid tamatar

SERVES 4

700g baby squid, cleaned

3 garlic cloves, peeled and chopped

2.5cm ginger, peeled and chopped

1 small onion, peeled and roughly chopped

2 tbsp vegetable oil

2 tbsp malt or cider vinegar

1 tsp ground cumin

1 tsp ground turmeric

6 black peppercorns, freshly crushed

1 tsp sea salt, or to taste

¼ tsp ground nutmeg

¼ tsp ground cloves

400g ripe plum tomatoes, skinned and chopped

1 cinnamon stick

2 bay leaves

freshly ground black pepper

Hyderabad, the capital of Andhra Pradesh, has a 400-year-old culinary history, which has produced a cuisine that is a blend of Moghlai and Persian cooking. Tomatoes (*tamatar*) and black peppercorns feature largely in Hyderabadi cuisine. Both of these ingredients combine to create a delectable blend of flavours in this dish. The mouth-watering sauce also works well with fresh prawns, crayfish or meaty chunks of monkfish.

Pull out the tentacles from the main body of the squids then cut the body into halves. Set aside.

Put the garlic, ginger and onion in a food processor and blend to fine wet paste. If necessary, add a tablespoon of water to get an even blend. Heat the oil in a large pan over a medium heat and, when hot, add the wet paste. Cook for about 15–20 minutes, stirring frequently to prevent it catching and burning. When the onion paste is golden brown, add the vinegar and cook until the liquid has evaporated. Add the cumin, turmeric, crushed peppercorns, salt, nutmeg and cloves and gently fry for 2 minutes to allow the spices to cook out.

Add the tomatoes, cinnamon, bay leaves and 150ml water. Cover and simmer for about 45 minutes. Add the squid, stir and gently simmer, uncovered, for 5 minutes, until it is just cooked through and tender.

Ladle into a warm serving bowl, grind over a little black pepper and serve immediately.

SERVES 4

500g skinless and
 boneless monkfish
 tails
¼ tsp ground turmeric
½ tsp sea salt, or to taste
juice of 1 lime
2 tbsp vegetable oil
1 large onion, peeled
 and finely chopped
3cm ginger, peeled and
 finely grated
3 garlic cloves, peeled
 and finely crushed
3 green chillies,
 deseeded and slice
 in half lengthways
4 curry leaves
½ tsp sea salt
400ml tin coconut milk
6 cherry tomatoes,
 quartered
handful of coriander
 leaves, to garnish

Monkfish moilee

Meen or fish moilee is a simple coconut fish curry from Kerala on the west coast of India. Some consider it an Anglo–Indian dish as it was commonly found in other Southeast Asian cuisines connected through the British empire. Meaty and robust monkfish tails are ideal for this curry, but you can also choose to use more delicate sea bass or haddock fillets. If using the latter, try not to stir the curry too much to prevent the fish breaking up during cooking.

Cut the monkfish tails into bite-sized chunks and place in a bowl. Mix together the turmeric, salt and lime juice to create a wet paste then mix this with the monkfish chunks and leave to marinate for about 20 minutes.

Heat the oil in a large heavy-based pan over a medium-to-high heat. Add the onion, ginger, garlic, chillies, curry leaves and salt. Stir frequently for 5–6 minutes until the onion is translucent and soft. Pour in the coconut milk and bring to a gentle simmer, stirring occasionally. Add the marinated fish and cherry tomatoes. Gently simmer for another 4–5 minutes until the fish is cooked through.

Ladle the curry into a warm serving bowl and garnish with coriander leaves. Serve with plain basmati rice.

SERVES 4

500g tuna steaks

sea salt and freshly
  ground black pepper

3 tbsp coconut or
  vegetable oil

3 garlic cloves, peeled
  and finely chopped

3cm ginger, peeled and
  finely shredded into
  matchsticks

1 tsp hot chilli powder

½ tsp ground turmeric

½ tsp fenugreek

2–3 tsp tamarind paste,
  to taste

150g finely grated
  coconut (optional)

1 red chilli, halved
  lengthways, with seeds
  removed if you prefer

200ml water

6–8 curry leaves

1 tsp black mustard
  seeds

Tuna vattichathu

This is another popular fish dish from Kerala. The curry is usually cooked with oily fish such as sardines and mackerel in an earthenware pot called a *chatty*. For a less greasy finish I'm using fresh tuna, which tastes fantastic in the hot and spicy sauce. Traditionally, *kokum* (made from dried mangosteen peel) is used as a souring agent for this dish, but as it is difficult to source in the UK I'm using tamarind paste instead.

Cut the tuna into bite-sized pieces and mix with a little salt and pepper. Set aside.

Heat 2 tablespoons of oil in a wide pan and fry the garlic, ginger, chilli powder, turmeric and fenugreek. Stir-fry for a few minutes until the paste is fragrant. Add the tamarind paste, grated coconut, if using, and red chilli and stir-fry for a couple more minutes.

Pour in the water and bring to a gentle simmer. Add the tuna to the pan and stir well to coat in the sauce. Simmer gently for 3–4 minutes until the fish is just cooked through. Taste, adjust the seasoning, then transfer the curry to a warm serving bowl.

Heat the remaining oil in a small saucepan and fry the curry leaves and mustard seeds over a medium heat for 1–2 minutes until fragrant and the mustard seeds begin to sputter. Tip the curry leaves, seeds and oil over the curry and give it one or two stirs. Serve immediately with steamed rice or warm Indian breads.

Goan fish ambotik

This sour and fiery fish curry comes from Goa, and it is popular among the Catholics in the region. It is widely thought that the dish has Portuguese–Indian origins, because *ambot* indicates 'sour' and *tik* means 'spicy' in Portuguese. This is also exemplified by the typical Portuguese practice of using vinegar in cooking. The curry is commonly made with shark or skate caught along the western Indian coastline, but use any firm-fleshed fish, such as kingfish, monkfish, halibut or tuna, or even an oily fish like mackerel, cut across the bone into steaks.

Cut the fish into bite-sized chunks and place in a large bowl with the tamarind paste and a little seasoning. Mix well and set aside to marinate while you prepare the rest of the dish.

To make the hot and sour chilli paste, place all the ingredients in a food processor and blend to a fine wet paste. If necessary, add a tablespoon or two of water and scrape down the sides of the bowl a few times to get the paste evenly ground.

Heat the oil in a wide pan and add the onion and some seasoning. Stir frequently over a medium-to-high heat for 6–8 minutes until the onion is translucent, soft and lightly browned. Tip in the chilli paste and fry for another couple of minutes until fragrant. Add the fish pieces to the pan and stir gently to coat in the sauce. If the sauce seems too dry, add a splash of water. Simmer for 3–4 minutes until the fish is just cooked through. Taste and adjust the seasoning. Serve garnished with some coriander leaves and plenty of plain basmati rice.

SERVES 4

500g firm-fleshed fish
  (see intro left)
1½ tbsp tamarind paste
sea salt and freshly
  ground black pepper
1 tbsp vegetable oil
1 large onion, peeled
  and finely chopped
handful of coriander
  leaves, to garnish

**HOT AND SOUR
CHILLI PASTE**

6 red chillies, deseeded
  and roughly chopped
1 tsp cumin seeds
½ tsp black peppercorns
2.5cm ginger, peeled
  and chopped
3 garlic cloves, peeled
  and chopped
2 tsp malt or cider
  vinegar
1 tsp caster sugar

Dry crab curry

SERVES 4

I am partial to cooking crab on the shell because I find that food tastes especially delicious when you're forced to use your fingers and 'work' for little bites of pleasure. This curry only requires half the effort as it is far easier to extract the flesh from meaty crab claws rather than from the body of whole small crabs, which is what they would use in India. Enjoy the curry with some plain steamed rice.

Crack the crab claws by tapping them with the back of a strong cleaver, heavy pestle or rolling pin. Set aside.

Heat the oil in a large pan or wok and fry the fenugreek, fennel seeds and curry leaves for 1–2 minutes until they become very aromatic. Add the ginger, garlic and onions and fry for 6–8 minutes, stirring occasionally, until the onions have softened and lightly browned. If the mixture starts to stick to the bottom of the pan, add a little splash of water.

Add the chilli powder, coriander, turmeric and salt to the pan and stir well. After a minute or two, add the chopped tomatoes. Continue to fry until most of the liquid has been cooked off and the pan is quite dry. Stir in the crab claws and leave to simmer for 4–6 minutes, until heated through.

Meanwhile, dry-roast the grated coconut in a hot pan for 3–4 minutes or until it turns golden brown. Sprinkle the toasted coconut on top of the curry and stir well. Transfer to a warm bowl and serve immediately.

SERVES 4

1kg cooked crab claws, thawed if frozen
3 tbsp vegetable oil
½ tsp fenugreek, crushed with a pinch of salt
1 tsp fennel seeds
6 curry leaves
2.5cm ginger, peeled and finely grated
6 garlic cloves, peeled and finely chopped
4 onions, peeled and finely chopped
1 tsp hot chilli powder
2 tsp ground coriander
1½ tsp ground turmeric
½ tsp sea salt, or to taste
4 tomatoes, peeled and roughly chopped
100g grated coconut

Grilled snapper with dry spices

This is one of the easiest and quickest ways to cook fish, using what I would consider storecupboard ingredients. The dry spice paste is wonderfully aromatic and really enhances the flavour of the fish.

First, make the dry spice paste. Place a frying pan over a medium heat and carefully roast the coriander, fennel and cumin seeds. Tip into a small bowl and add the garlic powder, salt, sugar and paprika. Stir in the lemon juice and vegetable oil and whisk together until well combined.

Preheat the grill to the highest setting. Rub the dry spice paste all over the snapper fillets then place on a lightly oiled baking tray, skin-side up. Cook the fish under the hot grill for about 5 minutes until firm and just cooked through. Serve immediately with some lime wedges to squeeze over.

SERVES 4
4 red snapper fillets,
  each about 150–170g
lime wedges, to serve

DRY SPICE PASTE
2 tsp coriander seeds
2 tsp fennel seeds
1 tsp cumin seeds
1 tsp garlic powder
1 tsp sea salt
2 tsp caster sugar
2 tsp ground paprika
1–2 tbsp lemon juice,
  to taste
1½ tbsp vegetable oil

Crispy battered fish with spiced okra and aubergine

SERVES 4

4 Dover sole fillets, about 150g each
30g rice (or plain) flour
½ tsp ground turmeric
sea salt and freshly ground black pepper
vegetable oil, for deep-frying

FISH BATTER

100g plain flour
100g rice flour
generous pinch of sea salt
½ tsp baking powder
300ml cold beer
2 large egg whites

This is not an authentic Indian dish but one I created as part of a recipe challenge. It features *karimeen*, which is a fantastic fish that is unfortunately unavailable for British consumption. As this recipe is very loosely based on our much loved battered fish back home (without the chips!) you can use any white fish that you might find on offer at your local fishmonger. I've chosen Dover sole here, for its silky smooth and delicate flesh, but a less expensive variety of the sole family would work just as well.

Pat the fish fillets dry with kitchen paper, then trim the fillets to about 8–10cm each. Mix together the flour and turmeric and season with a pinch each of salt and pepper. Lightly dust the fish fillets in the flour mixture and shake off any excess.

To make the batter, sift the flours, salt and baking powder together in a large bowl. Whisk in enough beer to make a loose batter. In a separate bowl, whisk the egg whites together until they form stiff peaks. Fold the egg whites into the batter to combine, adding any extra beer if necessary to loosen the mixture. Set aside.

Heat the oil in a deep-fat fryer to 180–190°C. Deep-fry the okra in the hot oil, in batches, for 2–3 minutes. Remove and drain on kitchen paper. Once cool enough to handle, cut the okra into approximately 1.5cm pieces. Deep-fry the aubergine in batches for 1–2 minutes. Remove and drain well on kitchen paper. Set aside. Reserve the oil.

Meanwhile, heat the coconut or vegetable oil in a large pan and sauté the shallots with the cumin seeds, cinnamon, star anise, cloves, turmeric and a pinch each of salt and pepper. Sauté for a few minutes until the shallots have softened. Add the okra and aubergine to the pan and continue to cook for another 4–5 minutes, stirring frequently until the mixture has softened. Stir in the coriander and check the seasoning. If necessary, drain the mixture through a sieve placed over a bowl to drain away any excess oil. Remove the star anise and discard. Keep warm.

To fry the fish, dip each fillet into the batter and then lower into the reserved hot oil. Cook in batches for 2–3 minutes or until golden brown. Drain on kitchen paper.

Put neat dessertspoonfuls of the spiced okra and aubergine mixture on each warm serving plate. Top with the crispy battered fish and serve at once.

SPICED OKRA AND AUBERGINE

200g okra, trimmed
1 large aubergine, diced into 1.5cm pieces
2 tbsp coconut or vegetable oil
3 shallots, peeled and finely sliced
2 tsp cumin seeds, toasted
1 tsp ground cinnamon
1 star anise
¼ tsp ground cloves
¼ tsp ground turmeric
handful of coriander, leaves chopped

Mackerel masala

Poultry & meat

Chilli beef fry

Chicken palak

Lamb korma

Spiced pan-fried chicken with pumpkin purée

Punjabi masala chops

Butter chicken

Guinea fowl in tomato and coconut curry

Chicken badami

Malabar duck

Spiced leg of lamb wrapped with spring onions

Tribal chicken casserole with tamarind

Quail tandoori

Chicken and papaya curry

Venison stew

Chilli beef fry

This is my version of the chilli beef fry I sampled in one of the many toddy shops along the Kerala coast. A toddy shop is a scaled-down Indian equivalent of our local pub, and a toddy is a potent drink made from the fermented sap of a palm or coconut tree. It packs a mean punch due to the high alcohol content. There is little doubt in my mind that the hot, spicy and salty chilli beef fry is served to encourage more drinking from the punters. I've toned down the dish slightly to make it a little more balanced and omitted the toddy, which is difficult to find here, to say the least. Serve it with plain rice, a side vegetable, some cooling raita and a sweet chutney.

Cut the beef into thin strips and put it into a large dish with half the chilli powder, the chilli flakes, dried mango powder, ginger and some seasoning. Add the coconut oil, if using, and mix well. Let the meat marinate for 15–20 minutes before cooking.

Heat a tablespoon of oil in a pan and add the onion, chillies, remaining chilli powder and a pinch of salt. Cook, stirring every now and then, for 5–6 minutes until the onion is soft and translucent. Add the sugar and fry for a few more minutes until the onion begins to caramelise. Add the lime juice and take the pan off the heat.

Heat 5cm of oil in a deep pan until hot. Toss the beef in the flour until evenly coated then deep-fry in batches for 2–3 minutes until brown and crisp. Drain on a plate lined with kitchen paper. When all the beef has been cooked, toss the strips with the onion mixture and sliced chilli. Transfer to a warm plate and serve immediately.

SERVES 4
600g beef fillet
1 tsp hot chilli powder
pinch of chilli flakes
1 tsp dried mango powder
3cm ginger, peeled and grated
sea salt and freshly ground black pepper
1 tsp coconut oil (optional)
vegetable oil, for deep-frying
1 large onion, peeled and very finely chopped
2 dried red chillies
1 tsp caster sugar
juice of 2 limes
3 tbsp rice or corn flour
1 fresh red chilli, deseeded and thinly sliced

SERVES 4

500g boneless and
  skinless chicken
  thighs
sea salt and freshly
  ground black pepper
400g spinach leaves
2 tbsp ghee or melted
  unsalted butter
2 bay leaves
3 cloves
6–8 black peppercorns
1 cinnamon stick
1 tsp cumin seeds
1 large onion, peeled
  and thinly sliced
2 garlic cloves, peeled
  and grated
2cm ginger, peeled and
  grated
2 green chillies,
  deseeded and finely
  chopped
1 tsp mild chilli powder
½ tsp ground turmeric
1 tsp ground coriander
2 large tomatoes,
  skinned and chopped
½ tsp garam masala

Chicken palak

This mildly spiced curry is a great introduction to Indian food. It's a healthy dish, and with a sauce made from spinach it's a great way to get kids to eat their greens, though you may want to adjust the amount of chillies and chilli powder used accordingly. I like to brown the butter for the sauce to create a nutty flavour to complement the earthy spinach. I've also chopped half the blanched spinach to give the dish a varied texture, but you may wish to purée the whole lot to stop fussy young children picking it out.

Cut the chicken into bite-sized pieces and mix with a pinch each of salt and pepper. Set aside.

Bring a large pan of salted water to the boil, add the spinach and blanch for 2–3 minutes. Drain well. Tip half of the spinach into a food processor and blend to a smooth purée. Finely chop the remaining spinach and set aside.

Place a large non-stick pan over a low heat, add the ghee or butter and cook until it turns a light brown colour, but do not let it burn. Add the bay leaves, cloves, black peppercorns, cinnamon and cumin seeds. Fry for a minute or until the spices become very aromatic.

Spiced pan-fried chicken with pumpkin purée

I made up this elegant dish as a way to thank food writer Seema Chandra after she kindly set me up on my first-ever journey across several north-western states in a quest to discover true Indian food. When I got back to New Delhi I wanted to cook her and her friends something special, but there was no point in cooking a truly authentic Indian meal since she can easily get that every day. This dish is the result of what I'd learnt from that epic trip, with one or two European cooking tricks thrown in for good measure. For example, I created a lovely aromatic sauce (not illustrated) made with chicken stock, an ingredient not generally used in Indian cooking. If you wish to cook this for a dinner party, prepare the different elements (i.e. make the pumpkin purée and sauce and marinate the chicken) so that you only need to cook the chicken and reheat everything just before serving. My Spiced aubergine and okra sauté (see page 146) is the perfect vegetable accompaniment for the chicken.

First, marinade the chicken. Put the chicken pieces into a large bowl and rub all over with a little salt and pepper. In another bowl, combine the papaya, cloves, cumin, turmeric, sugar, ginger, lime and orange juices and yoghurt, then add this to the chicken and toss well to coat. Cover the bowl with cling film and marinate in the fridge for at least a couple of hours.

SERVES 4

1 whole chicken, jointed into 8 pieces
sea salt and freshly ground black pepper
2 tbsp finely grated raw green papaya
½ tsp ground cloves
1 tsp ground cumin
½ tsp ground turmeric
1 tsp caster sugar
1 tsp finely grated ginger
juice of 1 lime
juice of 1 orange
200ml natural yoghurt
2–3 tbsp corn flour
½–1 tsp hot chilli powder, to taste
vegetable oil, for frying
1 large hard-boiled egg, soaked in 2 tbsp water with a pinch of saffron added (optional)

Punjabi masala chops

Punjabi cooking is perhaps the Indian cuisine with which we are most familiar, as the vast majority of Indian restaurants in Britain offer food from this region. This style of cooking favours dishes that use tomatoes, and in this recipe they form an integral part of the sauce. Although not traditional, I prefer to seal off the chops before adding them to the sauce so they caramelise and add a meaty, savoury flavour.

Trim off any excess fat around the chops, leaving on a thin, even layer, and season well. Put the ginger, garlic, chilli and a tablespoon or two of water into a food processor or blender and blitz to wet paste. Heat 2 tablespoons of oil in a wide, heavy-based pan, and when you can feel a strong heat rising, add the lamb chops and fry for about 1–2 minutes on each side, until lightly browned all over. Remove the chops from the pan and set aside.

Add the remaining oil to the pan and add the onions, garam masala, cumin, cayenne pepper and chilli powder. Stir well and sauté gently for 3–4 minutes or until the onions have softened slightly and the spices are fragrant. Add the ginger and garlic paste and cook for another couple of minutes. Increase the heat and add the browned chops, tomatoes, lemon juice and salt. Bring to the boil, then reduce the heat to a simmer and partially cover the pan. Simmer, stirring occasionally, for 50 minutes–1 hour or until the meat is tender and the sauce thick. Over a low heat, gradually stir in the yoghurt and simmer for a few minutes. Taste and adjust the seasoning.

Arrange the chops on a warm platter and garnish with coriander leaves. Serve immediately with warm breads or plain basmati rice.

SERVES 4

8 lamb chops
3cm ginger, peeled and
  roughly chopped
4 garlic cloves, peeled
  and roughly chopped
1 red chilli, deseeded
  and roughly chopped
3 tbsp vegetable oil
2 onions, peeled and
  finely chopped
2 tsp garam masala
1 tsp ground cumin
1½ tsp cayenne pepper
1 tsp mild chilli powder
800g chopped plum
  tomatoes
2 tbsp lemon juice
1 tsp sea salt, or to taste
450ml natural yoghurt
coriander leaves, to
  garnish

SERVES 4

800g boneless and
  skinless chicken
  thighs, cut into
  3–4cm pieces
2 garlic cloves, peeled
  and finely crushed
2cm ginger, peeled and
  finely grated
½ tsp fine sea salt
½ tsp hot chilli powder
1½ tbsp lemon juice
75ml natural yoghurt
½ tsp garam masala
½ tsp ground turmeric
1 tsp ground cumin
1–2 tbsp vegetable oil,
  for brushing

SAUCE

1½ tbsp ghee or melted
  unsalted butter
2 garlic cloves, peeled
  and finely chopped
2cm ginger, peeled and
  finely chopped
1 cardamom pod, seeds
  lightly crushed
2 cloves
1 tsp ground coriander
1 tsp garam masala
1 tsp ground turmeric
1 tsp hot chilli powder,
  or to taste
275ml tomato purée
1 tbsp lemon juice
40g unsalted butter
100ml double cream
1 tbsp chopped
  coriander, to garnish

Butter chicken

Butter chicken, or *murgh makhani*, was one of the first dishes I tasted when I went to India. Its origins can be traced back to Moghul times, but the dish and its history is most closely associated with Delhi's famous Moti Mahal restaurant, where I had the pleasure of eating this fantastic dish. Over time, numerous chefs have attempted to emulate the rich buttery sauce, and flavours vary slightly between restaurants. This is my version of the classic dish.

Place the chicken in a bowl with the garlic, ginger, salt, chilli powder and lemon juice. Mix, cover with cling film and chill for 30 minutes. Mix together the yoghurt, garam masala, turmeric and cumin and add to the chicken, making sure that each piece is well coated with the mixture. Cover again and chill for 3–4 hours.

Preheat the oven to 180°C/Fan 160°C/Gas 4. Put the marinated chicken pieces on a grill rack set on a baking tray and bake for 8–10 minutes. Brush the chicken pieces with a little oil and turn them over. Bake for another 10–12 minutes until just cooked through.

For the sauce, heat the ghee or butter in a pan and add the garlic and ginger. Fry for a minute or so then add the cardamom, cloves, coriander, garam masala, turmeric and chilli powder. Stir well and fry for 1–2 minutes until they give off a lovely aroma. Stir in the tomato purée and lemon juice and cook for another couple of minutes. Add the chicken pieces to the sauce and stir well to coat. Finally, add the butter and cream and stir continuously until the butter has melted and the sauce is smooth. Taste and adjust the seasoning. Transfer to a warm bowl and serve hot, garnished with chopped coriander.

Guinea fowl in tomato and coconut curry

Not surprisingly, this curry comes from South India, where the use of coconut and tomatoes is common-place. The Indians would use chicken, but guinea fowl breasts make a lovely alternative. Although it doesn't take long to prepare, this dish is best prepared ahead so that the guinea fowl has time to absorb the flavours of the curry. Reheat gently and serve with Coconut rice or a Plain dosa (see pages 169 and 194).

Cut the guinea fowl breasts into bite-sized pieces and rub all over with a pinch each of salt and pepper. Heat 2 tablespoons of oil in a large frying pan over a medium heat. In batches, fry the guinea fowl breasts lightly for 1–2 minutes on each side until lightly browned all over. Remove the meat from the pan to a plate as you brown each batch. Set aside.

Add the remaining oil to the same pan followed by the cinnamon, cloves and curry leaves. Cook for a minute or until the spices become very fragrant. Stir in the garam masala and chilli powder, and after 30 seconds add the onion and garlic. Sauté gently for 6–8 minutes until the onion is softened but not browned. Add the tomatoes and grated coconut, if using, then season lightly with salt and continue to cook for another 3–4 minutes.

Pour in the coconut milk and bring to the boil briefly. Reduce the heat and return the guinea fowl to the pan. Simmer for 5–10 minutes until the meat is just cooked through. Serve immediately.

SERVES 4

4 skinless guinea fowl breasts
sea salt and freshly ground black pepper
3 tbsp vegetable oil
½ cinnamon stick
¼ tsp ground cloves
4 curry leaves
1 tsp garam masala
1 tsp hot chilli powder
1 onion, peeled and finely chopped
2 garlic cloves, peeled and finely chopped
500g tomatoes, skinned and finely chopped
100g freshly grated coconut (optional)
400ml tin coconut milk

SERVES 6
large bunch long spring
  onions, about 10–12
4 large or 6 small ready-
  made chapattis
2.75kg leg of lamb,
  boned, butterflied
  and rolled
2 large banana leaves

MARINADE
4 garlic cloves, peeled
  and roughly chopped
2 tbsp ghee or melted
  unsalted butter
1 tsp sea salt, or to taste
1 tsp hot chilli powder
1 tsp ground coriander
1 tsp garam masala
1 large onion, peeled
  and roughly chopped
3 ripe plum tomatoes,
  roughly chopped
small bunch coriander,
  leaves and stems
  roughly chopped
juice of ½ lemon
  (or 2 tbsp ground
  kachri)

DRY SPICE RUB
1 tsp fine sea salt
1 tsp hot chilli powder
2 tsp garam masala

Spiced leg of lamb wrapped with spring onions

This is my modern take on a Rajasthani classic called *khud khargosh*, an ingenious recipe for pit-roasting meat in the desert using only natural resources: hot coals and desert sand. I was shown how to make the original recipe by the nephew of the Maharajah of Jodhpur and was told that the dish was traditionally made with hare (*khargosh*) until the hunting ban in the 1970s, which led to the popular use of goat or mutton. The original tenderiser for the meat came in the form of *kachri*, which resembles a small, yellowish-brown melon growing wild in the desert areas. Cooked fresh, kachri tastes of a mildly sour melon but it is also frequently dried and ground into a powder. It is rarely found outside of Rajasthan in either form, but I find that a little lemon juice provides a similar effect.

First, make the marinade. Put all the ingredients into a food processor and blend to a wet paste, stopping the machine to scrape down the bowl of the processor a few times. Transfer the paste to a bowl and set aside. In another small bowl, mix together the ingredients for the dry spice rub.

Lightly blanch the spring onions in a pan of boiling water for about a minute to soften them. Refresh under cold running water and drain well.

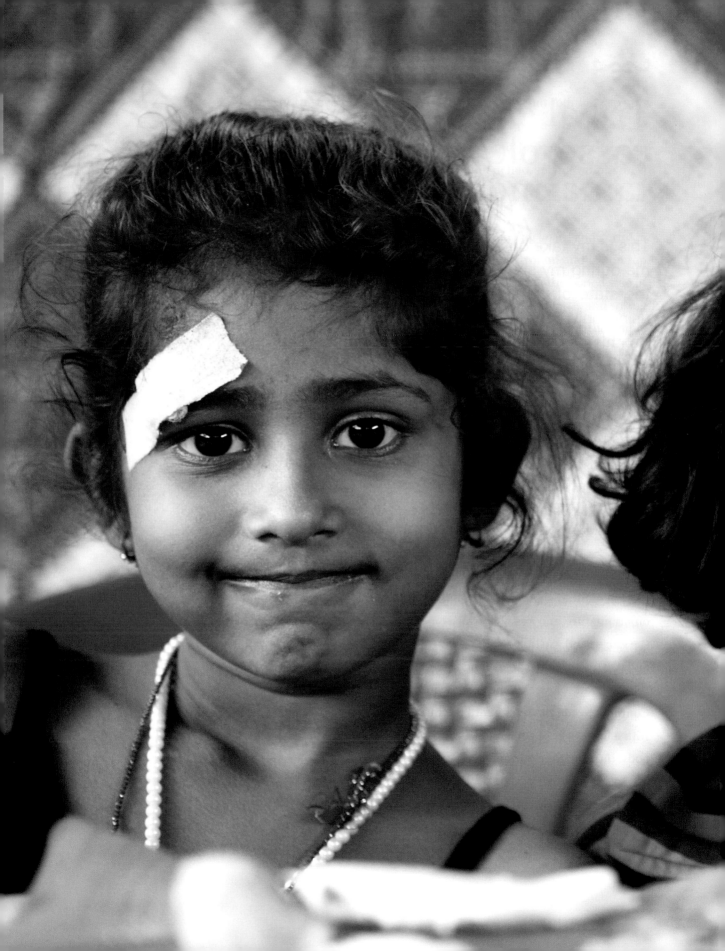

Quail tandoori

Tandoori chicken is probably one of the most recognised of all Indian dishes. The heat inside a proper tandoor is so intense that a whole marinated chicken can be baked in minutes to a succulent and moist finish, even though very little oil or fat is used. When using a domestic oven, you're more likely to get this result with small marinated quails. The secret is to marinate the birds for at least 4 hours or ideally overnight. I'm not a fan of using food colouring, but if you wish to add some to the marinade, please get a natural one. If you're serving this as part of a multi-course meal, one quail per person should suffice; otherwise serve two quails each.

Rub the quails with salt and place them in a large dish. Squeeze over the lemon juice, cover with cling film and chill for about 30 minutes.

Meanwhile, make the tandoori marinade. Put the ginger, garlic and onion in a food processor with a tablespoon of water and blitz to a fine wet paste. Tip into a large bowl and add the yoghurt, tomato purée, garam masala, chilli powder, paprika, cumin, coriander and food colouring, if using. Mix well. Coat the quails with the marinade and chill for 4 hours or overnight.

Preheat the oven to the highest setting. Remove the quails from the fridge and place on a baking tray, breast-side up. Coat with any remaining marinade and cook for 18–20 minutes or until just cooked through. The juices should run clear when you pierce the thickest part of each quail with a skewer. Serve with warm chapatti or naan breads and some sliced onions, tomatoes and lemon wedges.

SERVES 4
4–8 oven-ready quails
1 tsp sea salt
juice of 1 lemon

MARINADE
3–4cm ginger, peeled and chopped
4 garlic cloves, peeled and chopped
1 large onion, peeled and finely chopped
400ml natural yoghurt
1½ tbsp tomato purée
½ tsp garam masala
1 tsp hot chilli powder, or to taste
1 tsp ground paprika
1 tsp ground cumin
1 tsp ground coriander
a couple of drops each of natural red and yellow food colouring (optional)

SERVES 4

500–600g boneless
  and skinless
  chicken thighs
1 tsp ground turmeric
sea salt and freshly
  ground black pepper
2 tbsp mustard or
  vegetable oil
2 medium onions,
  peeled and finely
  chopped
3cm ginger, peeled and
  finely grated
3 garlic cloves, peeled
  and finely chopped
1 green chilli, deseeded
  and finely chopped
  (optional)
150ml water
6 tbsp finely chopped
  raw green papaya
juice of 1 lime
small handful of
  coriander leaves,
  to garnish

Chicken and papaya curry

This isn't so much a curry in the traditional sense of the word, but more like a light and flavourful casserole with chicken and papaya as the star ingredients. I cooked it as part of a recipe challenge upon returning from the northeast of India. The food there is lighter and the ingredients used are mostly fresh. The papaya acts not only as a tenderiser but also as a sauce thickener. If you prefer a smooth sauce, purée the papaya in a food processor instead of chopping it. I didn't add chilli in the original recipe, but I have included one as an option here, should you want a little heat in the curry.

Cut the chicken thighs into bite-sized pieces and mix them with the turmeric and some seasoning. Set aside.

Heat the oil in a wide heavy-based pan until hot. Add the onions, ginger, garlic and chilli, if using. Fry for 4–5 minutes, stirring frequently, until the onions begin to soften. Add the chicken pieces and mix well. Fry over a high heat for a few minutes then add the water and papaya and bring to a simmer. Cook gently for 15–20 minutes until the chicken is tender and the sauce is thick.

Finally, add the lime juice and seasoning to taste. Transfer to a warm serving bowl, garnish with the coriander leaves and serve while still hot.

Venison stew

I cooked this after an exhausting day hunting with the Konyaks, a tribe of hunters in Nagaland, at the northeastern tip of India. There was a ritual to the hunt and the butchering process. Tradition dictates that the deer's head and right thigh is given to the successful hunter and the left thigh is given to the chief. As an honoured guest, I was presented with the saddle (which, surprisingly, is not favoured over any other cut). The remaining parts were divided among the other hunters. I cooked the saddle at the communal kitchen, where I had at my disposal some fresh local vegetables, a little honey and a bottle of beer. (Dried spices are not common in this part of the world.) The resulting stew was a departure from the richly spiced curries that I'd been eating during the trip, but it was delicious and comforting.

Cut the venison into 2.5–3-cm pieces, then season all over with salt and pepper. Heat half the oil in a wide pan until hot. Fry the venison pieces in several batches for about 2 minutes on each side until browned all over. Transfer each batch to a plate and set aside. Put the remaining oil in the pan and fry the onions, carrots, chillies and garlic over a medium-to-high heat. Fry, stirring frequently, for 5–6 minutes until the vegetables soften. Add the flour and stir for about 2 minutes.

Pour in the beer and add the tomatoes, coriander stems and honey. Return the venison to the pan and simmer very gently for about 20 minutes until the venison is just cooked through and tender. Taste and adjust the seasoning. Just before serving, stir in the coriander leaves. Enjoy the stew with plenty of plain steamed rice.

SERVES 4

1kg boneless saddle of venison
sea salt and freshly ground black pepper
4 tbsp mustard or vegetable oil
2 onions, peeled and chopped
2 medium carrots, peeled and chopped
3 red chillies, deseeded and chopped
3 garlic cloves, peeled and finely chopped
2 tbsp plain flour
330ml bottle light beer
3–4 plum tomatoes, peeled and chopped
small bunch coriander, stems and leaves chopped separately
1½ tbsp honey, or to taste

Vegetarian

Rajasthani red lentil curry

Maharashtrian spiced cabbage

Mixed vegetable undhiyo

Andhra banana curry

Egg curry

Black-eyed bean curry

Spiced aubergine and okra sauté

Curried okra

Saag aloo

Cauliflower tandoori

Sweet potatoes with panch phoran

Stir-fried butternut squash with dried chilli

Spicy cucumber and coconut salad

SERVES 4

225g split pigeon pea
  lentils (tuvar dal) or
  red split lentils,
  washed
2 cloves
½ cinnamon stick
4 black peppercorns
1 litre water
2.5cm ginger, peeled
  and chopped
3 garlic cloves, peeled
  and chopped
3 tbsp ghee or melted
  unsalted butter
2 onions, peeled and
  finely chopped
3 tomatoes, skinned
  and finely chopped
2 tsp garam masala
2 tsp hot chilli powder,
  to taste
1 tsp ground turmeric
½ tsp sea salt, or to taste
2 tbsp double cream
3 green chillies, slit in
  half lengthways

Rajasthani red lentil curry

This dish is based on the lentil curry *dal baati*, a popular Rajasthani dish that in India is almost always served with baked round buns made from wheat and gram flours and ghee. I've chosen to leave out the *baati* buns to keep the recipe simple, and also because I think the curry is equally delicious eaten with plain naan or chapatti generously brushed with melted butter. You can make the curry with only one type of lentil (as I have) or use a mixture of tuvar (dark ochre-coloured split and skinned pigeon peas) and urad dals, although you may need to adjust the cooking times slightly, adding 15–20 minutes more.

Place the lentils in a saucepan with the cloves, cinnamon, peppercorns and water. Bring to the boil and skim off any scum and froth that rises to the surface of the liquid. Reduce the heat, partially cover the pan and simmer for 25–30 minutes until the lentils are soft and have broken down.

Put the ginger and garlic into a small food processor. Add a tablespoon of water and blitz to a paste. Heat the ghee or butter in a pan, add the onions and fry for 6–8 minutes, stirring occasionally, until lightly browned. Add the garlic and ginger paste, tomatoes, garam masala, chilli powder and turmeric to the pan.

After 2–3 minutes, tip the cooked lentils into the pan, season well with salt and leave to simmer for 8–10 minutes until thick. Stir through the cream and green chillies; then you are ready to serve.

Maharashtrian spiced cabbage

SERVES 4
500g green or
   white cabbage
2 tbsp vegetable oil
1½ tsp black mustard
   seeds
8–10 curry leaves
1½ tsp urad dal
1 large onion, peeled
   and finely sliced
½ tsp ground turmeric
1 tsp ground cumin
50ml water
sea salt, to taste
3 tbsp freshly grated
   coconut (optional)

This is a typical quick and easy vegetable stir-fry from Maharashtra, which goes well with pretty much any fish or meat dish. I particularly enjoy it with a biryani. It is also lovely as a side dish for roast meat – just think of our roast venison with spiced braised cabbage. For a variation, add a few nuggets of jaggery or light brown soft sugar and some fresh lemon juice to give the cabbage some sweetness and acidity.

Finely shred the cabbage and set aside.

Heat the oil in a wide pan over a medium heat. Add the mustard seeds and when they begin to pop, tip in the curry leaves and urad dal. When the urad dal begins to turn a light golden brown, after about 2–3 minutes, add the sliced onion and sauté gently for 6–8 minutes, or until soft.

Add the cabbage, turmeric, cumin, water and a generous pinch of salt to the pan. If you're using the grated coconut, add this now. Stir well and simmer for 5–7 minutes until the cabbage is cooked but still retains some bite. Taste and adjust the seasoning, then serve in a warm bowl.

SERVES 4

6–8 baby potatoes,
  peeled or just
  scrubbed, if you prefer
4–5 small Indian
  aubergines
  (or 1 medium),
  trimmed
1 small sweet potato
  (or yam), peeled
1 large carrot, peeled
1 large unripe banana,
  peeled
50g green beans, topped
  and tailed
2 tbsp vegetable oil
1 tsp mustard seeds
½ tsp carom seeds
¼ tsp asafoetida
  (optional)
½ tsp sea salt, or to taste
½ tsp ground turmeric
½ tsp ground cumin
½ tsp ground coriander
200ml water
small handful of toasted
  coconut shavings, to
  garnish (optional)

MASALA PASTE

4 garlic cloves, peeled
  and chopped
2.5cm ginger, peeled
  and chopped
3 green chillies,
  deseeded and chopped
75g grated coconut,
  thawed, if frozen
1 tbsp chopped
  coriander leaves

Mixed vegetable undhiyo

This tasty mixed-vegetable casserole originates from Gujarat in western India. It is mainly cooked in winter, but the ingredients may vary depending on what is available locally. I've sampled a couple of versions of the dish during my trip to India: one was wet with a thick greenish gravy; the other was a dry casserole of colourful vegetables, dry spices and grated coconut. This recipe is similar to the latter version, which I much preferred. Use any combination of vegetables you like, but do include several root vegetables to give the dish a hearty, starchy base.

First, make the masala paste. Put all the paste ingredients into a food processor. Add 3 tablespoons of water and blitz to form a thick paste.

Cut the potatoes, aubergines, sweet potato or yam, carrot and banana into bite-sized pieces, and the beans into 2cm pieces. Keep each ingredient separate.

Heat the oil in a large pan. Add the mustard seeds, carom seeds and asafoetida, if using. When the seeds begin to pop, add the masala paste. Cook for 2–3 minutes, stirring frequently. Put the potatoes and carrots into the pan and cook for 5 minutes before adding the rest of the vegetables, salt and the remaining ground spices. Fry over a high heat for 5 minutes, then reduce the heat, add the water and stir. Cover and simmer for about 10–15 minutes or until the vegetables are cooked through and tender. Transfer to a warm serving bowl and garnish with a sprinkling of coconut shavings, if you wish.

Andhra banana curry

Raw bananas regularly feature in Indian vegetarian dishes, and this exceptional curry is a must-try. It has well-balanced flavours with a warming heat from the spices, some sweetness from the bananas and a little acidity from the tamarind paste.

Put the garlic, ginger, urad dal and a splash of water in a blender or food processor and blitz to a fine wet paste. Scrape into a small bowl and set aside.

Heat the oil in a karahi or wok. Add the curry leaves and mustard seeds and cook for a minute until the seeds begin to splutter. Add the paste that you made earlier to the pan, along with the chilli powder and turmeric.

Fry the mixture for 4–6 minutes before adding the tamarind paste to the pan. Pour in the water and stir well. Bring to the boil, then reduce the heat and simmer for 2–3 minutes. Add the bananas to the pan and cook, stirring occasionally, for 6–8 minutes or until the sauce has thickened.

Transfer the banana curry to a warm bowl, stir in the coconut and serve immediately.

SERVES 4

4 garlic cloves, peeled and roughly chopped
3cm ginger, peeled and roughly chopped
1 tsp urad dal
2 tbsp vegetable oil
8 curry leaves
1 tsp black mustard seeds
1 tsp hot chilli powder
½ tsp ground turmeric
1½ tbsp tamarind paste
400ml water
6 large unripe bananas, peeled and cut into 4cm pieces
2 tbsp freshly grated coconut

SERVES 4

6 large eggs
1 tsp ground cumin
1 tsp ground coriander
1 tsp ground turmeric
1 tsp red chilli powder
½ tsp garam masala
1–2 tbsp water
2 tbsp vegetable oil
1 onion, peeled and
  finely chopped
400g tomatoes, skinned
  and chopped
1 tsp fine sea salt
handful of coriander
  leaves, roughly
  chopped

Egg curry

An egg curry is the ideal food for frugal times: it is tasty, economical and nutritious but, more importantly, it is a crucial source of protein for vegetarians. As this curry exemplifies, the Indians have a special flair for transforming something as basic as a boiled egg into a delicious dish. Serve with any type of Indian bread or plain rice, but I find Jeera or Tamarind rice make good accompaniments (see pages 186 and 166).

Put the eggs in a medium saucepan and cover them with cold water. When the water begins to simmer, set the timer to 10 minutes for hard-boiled eggs. Remove the eggs with a slotted spoon and cool them in a bowl of iced water. Drain, then gently peel away the shells. Slice them in half and set aside.

In a small bowl, mix together the ground cumin, coriander, turmeric, chilli powder and garam masala. Add enough water to create a wet paste with a slow-dropping consistency.

Heat the oil in a wide pan. Add the onion and fry for 6–8 minutes, stirring occasionally, until golden brown. Tip the spice paste into the pan and cook for 2–3 minutes before adding the chopped tomatoes and salt. Stir in the coriander and simmer for 4–5 minutes. If the sauce seems too dry, add a splash of water.

Carefully lower the boiled eggs into the pan and simmer gently until heated through, trying not to stir too much so that the egg yolks remain with the whites. When hot, transfer into a warm bowl and serve immediately.

Black-eyed bean curry

This is one of my favourite bean curries – it is very flavourful and you can eat it plainly with some rice or flat breads and a raita for a simple meal. From my travels I have acquired a neat Indian trick to make dried pulses easier to digest: leave them to soak well overnight and then cook them with a combination of ginger, turmeric (preferably fresh) and a little pinch of asafoetida.

Drain the soaked black-eyed beans and place them in a saucepan with the water. Bring to the boil and skim off the froth that rises to the surface. Reduce the heat to a simmer, partially cover and cook, stirring occasionally, until the beans are tender but not mushy. It should take about 30 minutes or so. Drain and set aside.

While the beans are cooking, heat the oil in a heavy-based pan and tip in the cumin seeds and cinnamon stick. When the spices are fragrant, add the onions and garlic. Fry for 6–8 minutes, stirring frequently, until the onions are soft and a dark golden brown. If they begin to burn, add a splash of water to the pan.

Add the ground cumin, coriander, cayenne pepper and a generous pinch of salt to the pan. Stir for a minute then tip in the chopped tomatoes and asafoetida, if using. Stir well, cover, and turn the heat down to a simmer. After about 10 minutes, add the cooked black-eyed beans and leave to simmer, uncovered, for a further 20 minutes. Taste and adjust the seasoning. Stir in the chopped coriander just before serving.

SERVES 4

250g dried black-eyed
 beans (*lobia*), soaked
 in plenty of water
 overnight
1.5 litres water
3 tbsp vegetable oil
1½ tsp cumin seeds
1 cinnamon stick
2 medium onions,
 peeled and chopped
4 garlic cloves, peeled
 and finely chopped
1½ tsp ground cumin
1 tsp ground coriander
1 tsp cayenne pepper
sea salt
350g tomatoes, skinned
 and chopped
pinch of asafoetida
 (optional)
2 tbsp chopped
 coriander

SERVES 4

1 medium aubergine
sea salt and freshly
  ground black pepper
1 tsp caster sugar
vegetable oil, for frying
1 large onion, peeled
  and chopped
1 tsp ground cumin
½ tsp ground turmeric
300g okra, roughly
  sliced
1 red chilli, deseeded
  and finely sliced
handful of mint leaves
handful of coriander
  leaves

Spiced aubergine and okra sauté

Before I went to India I had a great dislike for okra, or 'lady's fingers' – even going as far as banning it from my restaurants. I found its slimy texture unappealing and didn't think much of what it added to a cooked dish. After my trip I still can't say I've been converted to eating it regularly, but I am more open to cooking it in different ways. I created this dish to accompany to my Spiced pan-fried chicken with pumpkin purée (see page 109), and it has been very well-received, judging from the empty plates that came back.

Chop the aubergine into 1cm dice and place them in a colander. Toss with a generous pinch each of salt and pepper and the sugar. Leave them in the colander in the sink for about 20 minutes, by which time the salt will have drawn out some moisture from the aubergines.

Heat about 3cm of oil in a heavy-based pan until hot. Fry the aubergines for 2–3 minutes until soft. Remove with a slotted spoon and place in a sieve set over a bowl. Press down lightly with the slotted spoon to squeeze out the excess oil from the aubergines.

Pour out most of the oil from the pan, leaving about a tablespoon or so. Add the onion and some seasoning and fry for 5–6 minutes until translucent and soft. Add the cumin and turmeric and fry for a minute to toast the spices. Tip in the okra, chilli and aubergine and stir well. Cook for 2–3 minutes until the okra is just tender and the aubergines are hot. Season well to taste. Stir through the mint and coriander leaves, take the pan off the heat and serve immediately.

Curried okra

This is a dry okra dish and the trick is to stir-fry the vegetable quickly so that it gets cooked without too much moisture, which helps to prevent it becoming too slimy. A little acidity, in the form of lemon juice or tart tomatoes, also helps to reduce the sliminess of the finished dish. Young tender pods are best, as they do not require much cooking.

Place the garlic and chillies into a food processor or blender with 2–3 tablespoons of water. Blend to form a smooth paste. Scrape the mixture into a small bowl and add the cumin, turmeric and coriander. Wash the okra under running water and pat dry with kitchen paper. Trim away the stems just above the ridge and cut into 2cm pieces.

Heat the oil in a frying pan and add the paste that you have just made. Allow the spices to cook out for 4–5 minutes before adding the okra, salt, sugar and lemon juice. Stir well to coat the okra in the spices and stir-fry gently for 6–8 minutes, or until the okra is tender and the mixture is quite dry. Remove from the heat and serve immediately as part of a main meal.

SERVES 4–6

4 garlic cloves, peeled and roughly chopped
2 green chillies, deseeded and roughly chopped
2 tsp ground cumin
1 tsp ground turmeric
1 tsp ground coriander
400g okra
3 tbsp vegetable oil
1 tsp salt, or to taste
1 tsp sugar
juice of ½ lemon

SERVES 4

400g fresh spinach
leaves
2 tbsp vegetable oil
pinch of asafoetida
(optional)
1 tsp black mustard
seeds
1 tsp onion seeds
1 onion, peeled and
finely sliced
3 garlic cloves, peeled
and finely chopped
1 green chilli, deseeded
and finely sliced
600g floury potatoes,
peeled and diced into
2.5cm cubes
1 tsp sea salt, or to taste
½ tsp cayenne pepper
squeeze of lemon juice,
to taste

Saag aloo

This spinach (*saag*) and potato (*aloo*) dish is perhaps one of the most popular Indian side dishes in the UK. I certainly always ordered a portion with my Friday-night curries. It is ideal eaten with rice, a lentil dal and another vegetable, meat or fish main course.

Bring a pan of salted water to the boil. Add the spinach and blanch for a minute. Drain in a colander and refresh under cold running water. With the spinach still in the colander, use a large spoon to squeeze out the excess liquid. Lay the leaves out on a chopping board and chop coarsely. Set aside.

Heat the oil in a large frying pan. Add the asafoetida, if using, and the mustard and onion seeds. When the seeds begin to pop, add the onion, garlic and chilli. After 3–4 minutes, tip the diced potatoes into the pan and season with salt and cayenne pepper. Fry for a couple of minutes over a high heat, stirring frequently.

Add 4–5 tablespoons of water, cover and gently cook over a low heat for 20–30 minutes until the potatoes are tender, stirring or shaking the pan every so often so that the potatoes don't stick to the base and burn. If the mixture looks too dry, add a little more water.

Uncover the pan and add the blanched spinach along with the lemon juice. Give the mixture a stir then cook for 1–2 minutes until the spinach is heated through. Transfer to a warm plate and serve.

Cauliflower tandoori

Many Indian villages have community ovens where families can take their marinated meats, fish and vegetables to cook in blazing hot tandoors. This dish would literally take minutes to bake in a traditional tandoor, without the need to blanch the cauliflower beforehand (this prevents the vegetable drying out). This recipe achieves a similar result using a domestic oven, but you can also try grilling the cauliflower on a hot barbecue to add a slightly smoky element to the dish.

Blanch the cauliflowers in a pot of salted water for 2–3 minutes until barely tender. Drain and refresh in a bowl of iced water. Drain again.

In a large mixing bowl, combine all the remaining ingredients to make a marinade. Add the blanched cauliflower florets and toss well to coat. Place them on a lightly oiled baking tray and loosely cover with foil or cling film. Chill for a few hours to allow the flavours to infuse.

When ready to cook, preheat the oven to 200°C/Fan 180°C/Gas 6. Uncover the baking tray and place in the oven for 8–10 minutes until the cauliflower is golden brown and tender when pierced with a knife.

While the cauliflower is in the oven, fry the onion rings. Heat the oil in a pan until hot then add the onion rings, tomato purée and a pinch each of salt and pepper. When the onions are soft and golden brown, after about 6–8 minutes, and with the occasional stir, add the garam and chaat masalas. Stir well and fry for another minute. Take the pan off the heat and keep warm. Serve the cauliflower tandoori with the onions spread over the top and garnished with the coriander leaves.

SERVES 4

4 baby cauliflowers, trimmed and cut into large florets
300ml thick Greek-style yoghurt
3cm ginger, peeled and finely grated
3 garlic cloves, peeled and finely crushed
½ tsp sea salt, or to taste
½ tsp ground turmeric
1 tsp hot chilli powder, or to taste
1½ tsp garam masala
½ tsp ground coriander
1 tsp chaat masala

FRIED ONION RINGS

2–3 tbsp vegetable oil
2 onions, peeled and cut into rings
3 tbsp tomato purée
sea salt and freshly ground black pepper
1 tsp garam masala
½ tsp chaat masala
handful of coriander leaves, to garnish

SERVES 4

2 medium sweet
  potatoes
2 tbsp vegetable oil
1 tbsp ghee or melted
  unsalted butter
2 tbsp chopped
  coriander and 1 tbsp
  ginger, peeled and cut
  into matchsticks
  (optional), to garnish

PANCH PHORAN

1 tsp nigella or black
  onion seeds
1 tsp fennel seeds
1 tsp fenugreek seeds
1 tsp cumin seeds
1 tsp black mustard
  seeds

Sweet potatoes with panch phoran

You can buy a ready-made packet of panch phoran (an equal blend of five dried spices that is popular in Bengal) quite easily at Asian grocers. If, like me, you've already got a good selection of different spices in your kitchen cupboard, you may want to mix the blend yourself. I've listed the spices here should you choose to do so, but I would also suggest making up a large batch for storing so that you'll always have it to hand.

First, combine all the spices for the panch phoran and set aside. Peel the sweet potatoes and cut into 2cm dice. Blanch them in boiling salted water for 5 minutes, then drain well.

Heat the oil in a wide sauté pan. Add the panch phoran, and when the seeds start to crackle and pop, add the sweet potatoes. Stir well and sauté until the sweet potatoes are cooked through and browning slightly around the edges. Add the ghee or butter to the pan, and when it has been absorbed by the sweet potatoes, remove the pan from the heat.

Tip the potatoes into a warm serving bowl and sprinkle with chopped coriander and strips of ginger, if you wish.

Stir-fried butternut squash with dried chilli

SERVES 4
1 large butternut
  squash
2 tbsp vegetable oil
1 tsp cumin seeds
1 tsp onion seeds
2 garlic cloves, peeled
  and finely chopped
3–4 dried red chillies,
  deseeded and chopped
sea salt and freshly
  ground black pepper

I love the unfussiness of this dish and the fact that you can make a delicious plate of food with a handful of ingredients. Butternut squash is fantastic cooked this way, but the simple spicing would also work well with sweet potatoes, yam and pumpkin.

Peel the butternut squash, discard the seeds and cut into 2cm cubes. Blanch in boiling salted water for 5 minutes then drain well.

Heat the oil in a wide sauté pan. Add the cumin and onion seeds and fry for 30 seconds, then add the garlic. Sauté gently for a couple of minutes until the garlic is soft but not coloured.

Add the butternut squash and chillies to the pan and toss well to coat with the spices. Season well and cook for a further 4–6 minutes, until the butternut-squash pieces are tender and beginning to crisp slightly around the edges. Serve piping hot as part of a main meal.

SERVES 4

1 large cucumber
1 green or red chilli,
   deseeded and finely
   chopped
3 tbsp freshly grated
   (or toasted desiccated)
   coconut
2 tbsp lemon juice,
   or to taste
1 tbsp chopped
   coriander
2 tbsp salted peanuts,
   lightly crushed
1 tbsp vegetable oil
1 tsp mustard seeds
4–5 curry leaves
pinch of asafoetida
   (optional)

Spicy cucumber and coconut salad

This refreshing South Indian-style salad serves as a great accompaniment to any number of hot, fiery dishes. I also like to offer it alongside Indian starters, of which many are brown and deep-fried, to provide a hit of freshness and colour.

Peel the cucumber, cut it in half lengthways and scoop out the seeds using a spoon. Cut the flesh in half horizontally and then into long, thin strips using a swivel peeler or mandolin. Put the cucumber into a bowl and mix together with the chilli, coconut, lemon juice, coriander and peanuts.

Heat the oil in a pan and add the mustard seeds, curry leaves and asafoetida, if using. When they become fragrant (it should take less than a minute), remove from the heat and scatter over the salad. Mix well and serve.

Breads & rice

Goan mussel pilau

Puri

Tamarind or 'Festival' rice

Coconut rice

Coriander puris with chickpea masala

Vegetable pilau

Pilau rice with meatballs

Dum ba biryani

Chapattis

Parathas

Jeera rice

Chicken biryani

Naan

Peshwari naan

Plain dosa

Puri

These delicious puffed-up breads are often eaten for breakfast in northern India, and they are great served with lentil dal or a curry with a thick sauce. Puris are best eaten freshly cooked, but you can prepare the dough in advance and keep it covered in cling film to prevent it drying out. When ready to cook, heat the temperature of the oil until it is hot enough that each round of dough blisters and puffs up almost instantly. Serve immediately, as puris tend to deflate with time.

Sift the flour and salt into a large bowl. Add the ghee or butter and combine with your hands until the mixture resembles breadcrumbs. Add the warm water, a little at a time (you may not need all of it), until you get a stiff ball of dough. Tip the dough out on to a lightly floured surface and knead for 10 minutes or until smooth and well combined. Wrap the dough in cling film and set aside to rest for 30 minutes. Knead the dough once more on a lightly oiled surface. (Do not dust the dough with flour as the flour will burn easily when deep-frying.) Divide into 12 balls and roll out each ball into a thin round – about 10–12cm in diameter. Keep the dough rounds covered with cling film on a tray, in a single layer, until you are ready to cook them.

Heat 3cm of oil in a wide, deep frying pan (or a deep-fryer) to 180–190°C – to test the temperature, drop a piece of dough in the oil and it should brown in 10–15 seconds. Gently lower each round into the hot oil, one at a time. Initially it will sink to the bottom of the pan before blistering or puffing up and rising to the surface. When the bottom side is a light golden brown, after 1–2 minutes, turn it over to cook the other side for 10–20 seconds. Drain the puri on a tray lined with kitchen paper and cook the rest. Serve while still hot.

MAKES 12
200g atta or chapatti
   flour, plus extra to dust
½ tsp fine sea salt
2 tbsp ghee or melted
   unsalted butter
100–125ml warm water
vegetable oil, for deep-
   frying and greasing

SERVES 6

400g basmati rice
½ tsp fenugreek seeds
½ cinnamon stick
1 tsp black peppercorns
1 tsp cumin seeds
2 tsp coriander seeds
6 dried red chillies
4 tbsp coconut or
  vegetable oil
1 tsp mustard seeds
½ tsp urad dal
1 tsp channa dal
6 curry leaves
1 tbsp white sesame
  seeds
1 tbsp skinned peanuts
700ml water
1 tsp sea salt, or to taste
2 tbsp tamarind paste
15g jaggery, grated
75g freshly grated
  coconut
3 tbsp sesame oil

Tamarind or 'Festival' rice

Southern Indians love the distinct tanginess of tamarind rice, and it is immensely popular in Andhra Pradesh, Karnataka and Tamil Nadu (where locals refer to it as *pulihora*, *puliogare* or *puliyodharai* respectively). Tamarind rice is sometimes called 'festival rice' because it is served during most festivals in southern India, and it is generally cooked for worshippers to Hindu temples. I was shown how to make this dish in an ashram kitchen by four dynamic ladies, all of whom were staunch vegans and keen to show me the benefits of their diet and lifestyle. Although they were unsuccessful in converting me, I was truly impressed with the time, effort and detail that went into making every element of the tamarind rice. Admittedly, I have not been a fan of vegan food in the past, but this is one dish that I will make time and again.

Wash the rice in several changes of cold water then leave to soak for 30 minutes in fresh cold water. Drain well.

Place a dry frying pan over a medium heat. Tip in the fenugreek, cinnamon, black peppercorns, cumin, coriander and 4 dried chillies. Toast the spices for a minute, tossing them frequently, until they smell fragrant and are lightly golden brown. Tip them into a bowl and leave to cool, then grind to a fine powder using a spice grinder or pestle and mortar.

Coriander puris with chickpea masala

This recipe is based on *chole masala*, a Punjabi dish that is usually eaten with Indian breads as an afternoon snack or included as part of a meal. The chole is made with dried chickpeas, an important protein-rich pulse that is an essential part of the diet of India's numerous vegetarians. You need to soak the dried chickpeas in lots of water overnight so that they'll have enough time to swell to a third of their size before cooking. If you don't have time to make the coriander puris, simply serve the dish with store-bought plain puris or chapattis.

Place the chickpeas in a saucepan and pour over enough cold water to cover. Bring to the boil, then simmer for about 2 hours until they are very tender.

Next, make the puri dough. Sift the flour and salt into a large bowl, then stir in the coriander. Make a well in the centre and add the butter and warm water, a little at a time (you may not need all of it), until it forms a stiff ball of dough. Tip the dough out on to a lightly floured surface and knead for 10 minutes until smooth. Wrap it in cling film and leave to rest for about 20 minutes.

For the chickpeas, heat the oil in a karahi or large wok over a medium heat. Add the onions and stir frequently for 6–8 minutes until they are golden brown. Add the chillies, ginger and garlic and fry for 3–4 minutes, then add the tomatoes. Cook until the tomatoes have softened, then stir in the cumin, turmeric and garam masala.

SERVES 4–6

CHICKPEA MASALA
200g dried chickpeas, soaked overnight, rinsed and drained
2 tbsp vegetable oil
2 medium onions, peeled and finely chopped
2 green chillies, deseeded and finely chopped
3cm ginger, peeled and finely grated
2 garlic cloves, peeled and finely chopped
4 tomatoes, skinned and roughly chopped
½ tsp ground cumin
½ tsp ground turmeric
1 tsp garam masala

CORIANDER PURIS
200g chapatti or atta flour, plus extra to dust
½ tsp fine sea salt
3 tbsp chopped coriander leaves and stems
2 tbsp melted unsalted butter
about 100–125ml warm water
vegetable oil, for deep-frying

Drain the cooked chickpeas and add to the pan. Stir well and pour in about 150ml of water. Bring to a simmer and cook for 25–30 minutes or until most of the water has been absorbed.

Knead the puri dough briefly again, then divide into 12 balls. Roll out each ball into a thin round on a lightly oiled surface and layer them between sheets of baking parchment to stop them sticking together.

Heat 6cm of oil in a deep pan (or a deep-fryer) until very hot, about 180–190°C. Gently lower the dough balls, one at a time, into the hot oil and cook in several batches. The dough will sink to the bottom before puffing up and rising. With a metal spoon or spatula, spoon the hot oil over the puris to encourage them to puff up and blister. As one side turns golden brown, flip over the puri and cook the other side for 10–20 seconds. Remove the puri with a slotted spoon and drain on a baking tray lined with kitchen paper. Repeat until all the puris are cooked.

Ladle the chickpea masala into warm bowls and serve hot with the freshly cooked coriander puris.

SERVES 4–6

400g basmati rice

1 tbsp vegetable oil

2 tbsp ghee or melted
   unsalted butter

1 cinnamon stick

6 cloves

4 cardamom pods,
   lightly crushed

2 bay leaves

2 star anise

2 onions, peeled and
   finely sliced

1 tsp ground turmeric

1 tsp ground cumin

1 tsp ground coriander

1 tsp red chilli powder

sea salt

50g mushrooms, cleaned
   and roughly chopped

75g green beans

150g cauliflower, cut
   into florets

1 large carrot, peeled
   and finely chopped

100g peas, thawed if
   frozen

850ml water

30g raisins

30g toasted pistachio
   nuts

Vegetable pilau

In India, the fragrant rice for a pilau is usually cooked separately from the other ingredients and everything is mixed together at the end, similar to the way in which a biryani is made. This method ensures that all the elements in the dish are cooked to perfection; however, it is more time-consuming and requires a few extra steps. This recipe employs a simpler way of cooking everything in one pot. The pilau is delicious on its own, but I also like to serve it with a lentil curry or a meat-based dish for extra protein.

Wash the rice in several changes of cold water, then leave to soak in fresh cold water for at least 30 minutes. Drain well and set aside.

Heat the oil and 1 tablespoon of ghee or butter in a wide, heavy-based pan and add the cinnamon, cloves, cardamom, bay leaves and star anise. Fry for a minute until they begin to crackle and smell fragrant. Add the onions and fry for another 6–8 minutes, stirring frequently until soft and golden brown. Stir in the turmeric, cumin, coriander and chilli powder and fry the ground spices for another minute.

Add the remaining ghee or butter, a pinch of salt and all the vegetables to the pan. Sauté for 3–4 minutes then tip in the drained rice and stir well. Toast the rice over a high heat for a minute then pour in the water and add the raisins. Bring to a simmer, then cover and cook for about 10 minutes until the rice looks dry and the water has been absorbed. Turn off the heat and, without removing the lid, leave to steam for another 5 minutes. Uncover and fork through the rice and vegetables. Sprinkle with the toasted pistachios and serve.

SERVES 4
PILAU RICE
300g basmati rice
2 tbsp ghee or melted
   unsalted butter
1 tsp cumin seeds
4 cardamom pods
8 cloves
1 cinnamon stick
2 bay leaves
400ml water
1 tsp sea salt, or to taste

MEATBALLS
500g good-quality
   minced lamb
1 medium onion, peeled
   and finely chopped
2 garlic cloves, peeled
   and finely chopped
1 tsp garam masala
1 tsp ground cumin
½ tsp ground coriander
¼ tsp cayenne pepper
sea salt and freshly
   ground black pepper
2 tbsp chopped
   coriander leaves
3 tbsp natural yoghurt

Pilau rice with meatballs

It seems that every country in the world has a version of a meatball dish that is meant to be served with a starchy food such as rice or pasta. This aromatic rice and meatball recipe stems from a fusion of Persian and Indian cuisines. It is a delicious and warming meal and all you would need to serve alongside is a raita and a vegetable dish or light salad.

Wash the rice in several changes of cold water and then leave to soak for 30 minutes in fresh cold water. Drain well and set aside.

In a large bowl, mix together all the ingredients for the meatballs. Fry off a small ball of mixture to check the seasoning and adjust if necessary. With damp hands, divide the mixture into 12 equal-sized balls. Chill in the fridge for at least 30 minutes to allow them to firm up.

To make the sauce, put the garlic, ginger and tomatoes into a blender or food processor and blend to a fine wet paste. Tip the paste into a bowl and stir in the chilli powder, coriander, garam masala and the paprika. Set aside.

Heat a thin layer of oil in a large non-stick saucepan and carefully add the meatballs. Cook for 2–3 minutes until lightly browned on all sides. Remove from the pan and transfer to a warm plate. Add the bay leaves, cardamom pods and cinnamon stick to the same pan and cook for a minute, before stirring in the onion. Fry for 6–8 minutes until golden brown.

Chapattis

Chapattis (or *rotis*) are the staple food of northern India, where wheat is the main crop, and they appear in practically every meal. During my first few days in New Delhi, I felt quite inadequate at mealtimes as I watched fellow diners adeptly use small pieces of chapatti to scoop up a curry or dal. A chapatti is often referred to as a 'third hand' for this reason. In India, chapattis are cooked on a *tava*, a cast-iron flat plate that keeps a consistently hot temperature, but a cast-iron frying or griddle pan works just as well.

Sift the flour and salt into a large mixing bowl. Make a well in the centre and gradually add the water (you may not need all of it) and stir until the flour comes together to form a soft, cohesive dough. Tip the dough out on to a lightly floured surface and knead well until it forms a smooth ball. This should take about 8–10 minutes. Cover the dough with a damp tea towel and leave to rest for 30 minutes.

Lightly flour the work surface and your hands. Divide the dough into 12 equal-sized balls. Work with one ball of dough at a time (and keep the rest covered to prevent them drying out). Flatten the ball with your hands and then roll out to form a thin disc, about 12–15cm in diameter. Shake off the excess flour.

Heat a cast-iron frying pan or flat griddle over a medium heat. Lay the chapatti in the pan and cook for 1–2 minutes. When bubbles begin to form, flip it over and cook on the other side for a minute. To get it to puff up, hold it over a low open flame with tongs. When both sides are brown speckled, it is done. Remove and keep warm, covered with a clean tea towel, while you cook the rest. Serve immediately.

MAKES 12
250g atta or chapatti
   flour, plus extra to dust
1 tsp fine sea salt
150–200ml water

Chutneys & accompaniments

SERVES 4–6

1 tsp cumin seeds
1 small pomegranate
500ml natural yoghurt
3 tbsp chopped mint
  leaves
sea salt and freshly
  ground black pepper
squeeze of lemon juice

Pomegranate and mint raita

This pretty and refreshing raita is the perfect antidote to hot and fiery curries. You can also substitute the pomegranate seeds with half a cucumber that has been peeled, deseeded and grated.

Place a frying pan over a medium heat; add the cumin seeds and roast carefully for a minute or until the cumin begins to smell very fragrant. Remove from the heat and allow to cool completely before grinding the seeds to a powder in a pestle and mortar.

Roll the pomegranate on a hard surface, applying pressure with your hands in order to loosen the seeds. Cut the pomegranate in half and scrape the seeds out into a bowl. Try to avoid leaving on any of the bitter white pith.

Whisk the yoghurt briefly in a small bowl then add most of the chopped mint and pomegranate seeds, and the roasted cumin. Season to taste with salt, black pepper and lemon juice and mix well. Scatter over the remaining chopped mint and pomegranate seeds to garnish. Serve immediately or chill for later consumption.

**MAKES ENOUGH TO FILL
A 350ML JAR**

500g tomatoes

1 tbsp vegetable oil

1 tsp black onion seeds

4 curry leaves, roughly
  chopped

2 small onions, peeled
  and finely chopped

3cm ginger, peeled and
  finely chopped

100g caster sugar

200ml white wine
  vinegar

1 medium or ½ large
  cucumber, peeled and
  cut into fine dice

sea salt and freshly
  ground black pepper

Tomato and cucumber chutney

This lovely sweet-and-sour chutney has a jammy consistency but with extra texture from the addition of diced cucumber. It is fantastic served with Indian starters and meals, but I'm also partial to spreading spoonfuls of it on ham sandwiches. It is also a great way to make use of the summer glut of tomatoes.

To skin the tomatoes, lightly score the top and bottom of each tomato with a sharp knife. Drop the tomatoes into a pan of simmering water and blanch them for 40–50 seconds. Remove them with a slotted spoon and drop into a bowl of iced water to cool. Drain and peel off the skins before chopping the flesh into rough dice.

Heat the oil in a large pan and add the onion seeds and curry leaves. Fry for a minute or until the seeds begin to pop and splutter. Add the onions and ginger and sauté gently for 3–4 minutes until the onions have softened slightly. Add the sugar and vinegar, increase the heat slightly and stir to help the sugar dissolve.

Add the diced tomatoes to the pan, reduce the heat and simmer gently for 35–40 minutes, stirring frequently, until all the liquid released by the tomatoes has been absorbed and the mixture is tacky. If the chutney seems too runny, cook for a further 10–15 minutes. Add the diced cucumber to the pan, stir well to combine and cook for 2–3 minutes. Remove the pan from the heat and taste to check the seasoning, adding a little more salt and pepper as necessary. While the chutney is still hot, spoon into a sterilised jar (see page 206) and seal tightly. Keep in the fridge and consume within a month.

Sweets & drinks

Coconut burfi

Fruit salad with spiced syrup

Mango porridge

Gulab sharbat

Ginger fruit punch

Sweet yoghurt with saffron, cardamom and
   pistachios

Mango and mint lassi

Salty lassi with ginger and cumin

Almond halwa

Masala chai

Lightly spiced sesame and cashew nut cookies

Payasam

Gulab jamon

Cardamom and coconut-flavoured milk

Rasmalai

Rosewater kulfi

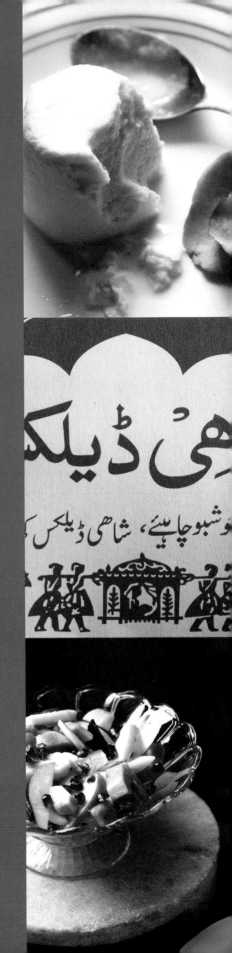

Sweet yoghurt with saffron, cardamom and pistachios

SERVES 4
1 litre thick Greek
  yoghurt
2 tbsp whole milk
generous pinch of
  saffron strands
150g icing sugar
2–3 cardamom pods,
  seeds finely ground
3 tbsp toasted pistachio
  nuts, roughly chopped

This is a very simple recipe that originates from western India. You can enjoy it plainly as a breakfast treat or dress it up with chopped nuts, caramelised orange slices and shredded mint leaves for an elegant dessert. For the latter, try substituting the cardamom with a little orange blossom water or rosewater. It is really worth leaving the yoghurt to hang in the fridge overnight so it becomes wonderfully creamy and dense.

Line a large sieve with muslin cloth or with several layers of kitchen paper and set it on top of a large bowl. Pour the yoghurt into the middle and leave to drain in the fridge for at least 4 hours or overnight. You can then pour off the drained whey in the bowl.

Warm the milk in a small pan (or in a small bowl in the microwave) and add the saffron strands. Remove the pan from the heat and leave to infuse for 20 minutes.

Tip the strained yoghurt into a bowl and sift in the icing sugar. Add the saffron milk, ground cardamom and 2 tablespoons of chopped pistachio nuts. Mix well and spoon into individual serving bowls or glasses. Chill, if not serving immediately.

Scatter the remaining chopped pistachios over the yoghurts just before serving.

SERVES 2

1 large or 2 medium
  ripe mangoes
250ml Greek yoghurt
200ml whole or semi-
  skimmed milk
1 tbsp caster sugar,
  or to taste
few sprigs of mint,
  leaves stripped
  (optional), plus extra
  sprigs to decorate
handful of ice cubes
  (optional)

Mango and mint lassi

This Indian-style smoothie is filling and refreshing at the same time. When in season during the summer, do use fragrant Alphonso or Kesar mangoes to make the lassi. Truly ripe ones can be so sweet that you may not need to add extra sugar to the drink. Mangoes differ in size, so do taste and add sugar as you go along.

Peel the mango(es) and carefully remove the flesh from the stone. Place in a blender with the yoghurt, milk and sugar. If you wish, add a few mint leaves to the mixture. Blend until light and fluffy. Taste and add more sugar if you think that it is needed.

Pour the lassi into two tall, chilled serving glasses and add the ice cubes, if you wish. Decorate with mint sprigs and serve immediately.

Salty lassi with ginger and cumin

SERVES 4
1 tsp cumin seeds
350ml natural yoghurt
1.5cm ginger, peeled
  and finely chopped
¼ tsp sea salt, or to taste
200ml ice-cold water

Throughout Asia a little salt is added to cooling drinks as a way to quench thirst and replenish lost moisture during hot and humid days. This salty lassi is not only refreshing but also very tasty and satisfying. Enjoy it on its own or with a light meal.

Place a dry frying pan over a medium heat. Add the cumin seeds and roast gently until the seeds begin to smell very aromatic. Remove from the heat and allow to cool before grinding to a powder in a spice grinder or with a pestle and mortar.

Pour the yoghurt into a blender with the ginger, salt and cumin powder. Blend well. With the motor still running, gradually pour in the water until you are happy with the consistency. (Lassi is generally served quite thick, but feel free to thin it down, if you prefer.) Taste to see if more salt is needed. Pour the lassi into tall serving glasses and serve at once.

Chai & Lightly spiced sesame cookies

SERVES 4–6

150g dried milk powder
75g plain flour
½ tsp baking soda
2 tbsp unsalted butter,
  melted
25–50ml whole milk
vegetable oil, for deep
  frying

SUGAR SYRUP

300g caster sugar
250ml water
2 tbsp rosewater

Gulab jamon

These balls are northern Indian versions of round doughnuts, except that they are made with milk powder and drenched in a fragrant rosewater- or cardamom-infused syrup. Sometimes a pinch of saffron is added to the syrup to give it a golden tinge. The dessert is now widely enjoyed all over the subcontinent and is usually eaten during festivals and special celebrations. *Gulab jamon* is best eaten warm but it is also delicious at room temperature. It is important to soak the balls in the syrup straight after deep-frying so that they remain tender and moist.

To prepare the sugar syrup, put the sugar and water into a saucepan over a medium heat. Stir continuously to help the sugar dissolve, then bring to the boil and reduce the heat. Simmer gently for 10 minutes until reduced and slightly thickened. Stir in the rosewater and remove from the heat.

Tip the milk powder, flour and baking soda into a large bowl and stir to combine. Make a well in the centre, add the butter and stir in enough milk to bring the ingredients together to form a stiff dough. Let the dough rest for 20 minutes.

Divide the dough into 18–20 pieces and gently roll each piece in your hands to form a smooth ball. (Do not roll the balls too firmly as you want them to have a soft and light texture when cooked.) Place the balls on a large plate and cover with a damp tea towel.

SERVES 4
2 litres whole milk
3–4 cardamom pods,
  seeds finely ground
130g caster sugar
1 tbsp rosewater
rose petals, to decorate
  (optional)

Rosewater kulfi

Kulfi is the name given to traditional Indian ice cream. As a street snack, it is frozen in little tube-shaped terracotta pots and sold by vendors called *kulfi-wallahs* from large vats filled with crushed salted ice. Needless to say, the variety of flavours sold by such vendors is endless, but for a light and refreshing dessert I really like the subtle taste and fragrance of rosewater kulfi. It can easily be made at home and has the added bonus of not requiring an ice-cream machine, although if you have one feel free to churn the kulfi mixture to get a lighter, airy texture.

Pour the milk into a wide heavy-based saucepan and slowly bring to the boil. Turn down the heat, stir in the ground cardamom and simmer for an hour or until reduced by half. The milk must be stirred frequently to prevent it catching on the base of the pan and burning. If a skin forms over the milk, don't worry, simply stir it back in.

Once the milk has reduced, add the sugar and rosewater. Continue to simmer, stirring constantly, for 2–3 minutes until the sugar has dissolved. Remove the pan from the heat and leave to cool completely, stirring every once in a while to prevent a skin forming.

Pour the cooled milk into four kulfi or dariole moulds. Cover the moulds with cling film and carefully transfer to the freezer. Freeze for at least 6 hours or overnight.

To unmould the kulfis, dip the moulds briefly in a bowl of warm water and invert on to shallow serving bowls. Decorate with rose petals, if you wish, and serve immediately.

Acknowledgements

This book would not have been possible without the support of my incredibly talented and dedicated team. First, I would like to thank Mark Sargeant and Emily Quah for their extraordinary dedication and their coordinated efforts in putting the book together, which include compiling and testing the recipes and styling the food for photography, Emma Lee and Jonathan Gregson for their amazing photography, Emma Thomas for her fantastic prop styling, Patrick Budge for designing yet another gorgeous and colourful book, and Emily Shardlow for her help with recipe testing.

My thanks also to the team at HarperCollins – Belinda Budge for her continued support; Hannah Black and Helena Caldon for their editorial work; and everyone involved in the production of this book.

I am also eternally grateful to the team at Optomen – from the dynamic Executive Producer, Pat Llewellyn, to the researchers, producers, cameramen, sound engineers and everyone else who worked tirelessly throughout the filming of the *Great Escape* episodes. My sincere gratitude also goes to all the remarkable individuals I met during my journey who have generously shared their time, knowledge and insights with me and shown me how to prepare truly wonderful, authentic and delicious Indian food.

My appreciation also to Jennifer Aves-Elliott, my PA, who has the admirable task of managing my diary and sorting out my life – a non-stop challenge not for the faint-hearted, I assure you. Also to my loving family and Chris Hutcheson for keeping me grounded and sane.

And finally, a special dedication goes to the late Alex Robinson – it was an honour to have known and worked with him and it would be an understatement to say that he will be deeply missed.